BUSINESS/SCIENCE/TECHNOLOGY DIVISION
CHICAGO PUBLIC LIBRARY
400 SOUTH STATE STREET
CHICAGO, IL 60605

QA
76.76
.C66
C48
2001

HWLCTC

Chicago Public Library

R0175930378

UML components : a simple process for sp

UML Components

D1402785

The Addison-Wesley Object Technology Series

Grady Booch, Ivar Jacobson, and James Rumbaugh, Series Editors
For more information check out the series web site [http://www.awl.com/cseng/otseries/].

The Component Software Series

Clemens Szyperski, Series Editor
For more information check out the series web site [http://www.awl.com/cseng/csseries/].

UML Components

A Simple Process for Specifying Component-Based Software

John Cheesman
John Daniels

Addison-Wesley

Boston • San Francisco • New York • Toronto • Montreal
London • Munich • Paris • Madrid
Capetown • Sydney • Tokyo • Singapore • Mexico City

Many of the designations used by manufacturers and sellers to distinguish their products are claimed as trademarks. Where those designations appear in this book, and we were aware of a trademark claim, the designations have been printed with initial capital letters or in all capitals.

The authors and publisher have taken care in the preparation of this book, but make no expressed or implied warranty of any kind and assume no responsibility for errors or omissions. No liability is assumed for incidental or consequential damages in connection with or arising out of the use of the information or programs contained herein.

The publisher offers discounts on this book when ordered in quantity for special sales. For more information, please contact:

Pearson Education Corporation Sales Division
One Lake Street
Upper Saddle River, NJ 07458
(800) 382-3419
corpsales@pearsontechgroup.com

Visit AW on the Web: www.awl.com/cseng/

LOC 000-61851

Copyright © 2001 by Addison-Wesley

All rights reserved. No part of this publication may be reproduced, stored in a retrieval system, or transmitted, in any form, or by any means, electronic, mechanical, photocopying, recording, or otherwise, without the prior consent of the publisher. Printed in the United States of America. Published simultaneously in Canada.

ISBN 0-201-70851-5
Text printed on recycled paper
1 2 3 4 5 6 7 8 9 10—CRS—0403020100
First printing, October 2000

BUSINESS/SCIENCE/TECHNOLOGY DIVISION
CHICAGO PUBLIC LIBRARY
400 SOUTH STATE STREET
CHICAGO, IL 60605

R0175930378

Contents

v

Foreword

Component software is finally taking off in a big way. Several companies now focus solely on resale, brokering, and consulting services around software components. Yet the practitioner is left with a confusing array of technologies and with mismatching methods and processes. Geared toward object-oriented analysis and design, the all-important component concept has fallen by the wayside in many object-centric approaches. Worse yet, there is the occasional thesis that components are special objects. Clearly, there is nothing wrong with objects—but it is components, not objects, that promise industrial leverage of software production and composition.

John Cheesman and John Daniels address the practical problem of architecting and specifying component-based systems head-on. This compact and very approachable text will help many who find themselves wedged between the need to utilize component technologies—currently mostly EJB and COM+—and the desire to apply the rich concepts of object modeling in general and UML in particular. Their pragmatic extension of UML captures important component concepts: component specifications, component interfaces, component implementations, and finally (generated by installed components) component objects. Only the last of these are objects.

Design by contract is the fundamentally simple and compelling idea to design systems as cooperating abstract boxes that achieve their common goal by relying on contracts. A contract specifies what each of the participants buying into collaboration has to do in order to benefit from the promised results. Contracts are formalizations of fair give-and-take among strangers and it is not surprising that a contractual approach is nowhere as natural as in a component world. Cheesman and Daniels take the formalization of contracts to the necessary level of precision, using the Object Constraint Language (OCL) that forms part of the UML foundation. Component specifications name the interfaces that a component adhering to the specification must implement.

Contracts enrich the operations of an interface with pre- and postconditions. However, the interface level does not constrain how components may interact. A typical example is a requirement that a component instance, whenever it receives a call on one of its interfaces, should then call a certain method of some other instance. Another common example is restrictions on the order in which operations on interfaces of a component instance may be called. Component specifications provide the required additional information.

The main contribution of this book, however, is a very workable process that builds on a clear conceptualization and rests on the author's extensive practical experience. John Cheesman and John Daniels have been drivers of the field for many years. This book is based on their experience with contributions to many influential methods and approaches and their application in practice. Readers will enjoy their direct, no-nonsense style as much as they will appreciate the many practical words of advice.

Clemens Szyperski, July 2000

Preface

This book describes how to architect and specify enterprise-scale component-based systems.

It is a practical and technical book. The business benefits of a component-based approach to building systems have been well documented in many theoretical books and we don't repeat these. Our focus is on helping people move from the theory to the detailed reality.

It seems to us that people who want to take a model-based approach to the design and construction of enterprise-scale component-based software face two big problems. First, what tasks and techniques can they use that will both produce a good system and be compatible with whatever project management process is in use? Little has been written to date about processes that can support the construction of large component systems. Second, how should they use the wide range of notations and techniques found in the Unified Modeling Language (UML)? The UML has become the de facto standard for pretty much all application development modeling, but its application to component-based approaches isn't obvious.

If you flick through the pages it might seem to you that we've concentrated mainly on the second of these problems—there are lots of UML diagrams—but a deeper examination will show, we hope, that the primary emphasis is on explaining a simple process by which components can be identified and specified, and robust but flexible application architectures can be produced.

Of course, the full development process covers more than just specification; it covers all activities from requirement gathering to system deployment. But this book focuses on specification. It explains how to represent requirements in a way that will facilitate the construction of specifications, it shows how to create specifications, and it gives guidance on implementing the specifications in software. We make no apology for focusing on specification. The main challenge that a component approach can meet is dealing with change, but the substitutability of parts this requires can be achieved only if components are properly specified.

Underpinning the process are a set of principles and definitions that organize and structure our thinking about software components. We have found these ideas to be a great help, and we urge you to take the time to understand and appreciate them. You'll find them set out in Chapter 1.

Who Should Read This Book?

We have written this book for practitioners—people who need to architect systems and specify components in UML today, using today's tools. We describe a clear process for moving from business requirements to system specifications and architectures. This will be helpful for those struggling with business-IT alignment in today's e-business world. The architecture pieces will assist those focusing on system architectures and assemblies, from city planning through detailed application architectures. The emphasis on unambiguous interface specification will be useful for those trying to establish software factories, those defining clear buy-and-build software policies, and those involved in application integration and legacy migration. It should also appeal to testing and validation teams.

We also think this book contains sufficient conceptual clarity and succinct explanations of techniques to make it of interest to both academics and educators. We certainly hope they will buy it.

How Best to Read This Book

Start at page 1 and keep going. When you reach a page that's thicker than the rest and shiny on one side, you're done. Seriously though, this isn't a big book, and we think you'll get most from it if you read it all. We think it's all important, so we can't suggest sections to skip on first reading, although you might find it useful the first time through only to skim some of the detailed specification examples, especially in Chapter 7. In fact, we tried to write the kind of book we like to read ourselves—lean and mean, with no unnecessary asides to distract from the main message.

Having read it all once, however sketchily, you will probably want to dip in and out of particular chapters as you're dealing with specific issues on your projects.

If you want to dig deeper into the examples we have provided, you can find the full case study at *http://www.umlcomponents.com*.

Where Did These Ideas Come From?

We'd like to think that the ideas in this book are all our own, but they're not. The component concepts and the process ideas we've used have been formed over a number of years and derive from a great many sources. We've relied heavily on the expertise of others who have struggled with—and solved, at least partially—related problems.

On John Cheesman's side the ideas come from his early work on the Microsoft Repository Open Information Model (OIM), in the mid-1990s; his work with Desmond D'Souza and Alan Cameron Wills on the Catalysis meta-model [D'Souza99]; UML, of course, to which he was a direct contributor; and Sterling Software's Advisor method for component-based development [Advisor], developed mainly by John Dodd and itself influenced by Catalysis.

John Daniels is one of the pioneers of object-oriented concepts and practices. In the early 1990s he developed, together with Steve Cook, the Syntropy method [Cook94]. This work has been a forerunner and common ancestor of many of the later developments mentioned above, especially Catalysis. The UML's Object Constraint Language (OCL) is directly descended from Syntropy, and several ideas first seen in Syntropy have found their way into the UML.

Figure P.1, although inevitably a simplification, gives some insight into how the ideas have influenced each other. Of course each of these areas

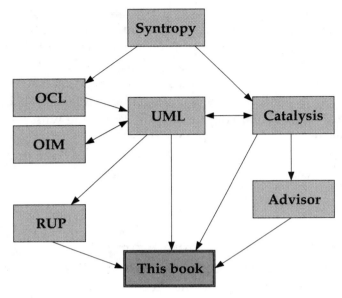

Figure P.1 Family tree

has its own set of influences, which we haven't shown, although OMT [Rumbaugh91] and Bertrand Meyer's notions of design by contract [Meyer00] deserve special mention.

We joined forces in 1999 to refine the concept models, tighten the process ideas, and align them with the workflows and terminology of the Rational Unified Process (RUP) [Jacobson99]. This book is the result.

Practical Experience

We have greatly benefited from studying the experiences of the Sterling Software component-based development (CBD) Customer Advisory Board (CAB). This is a set of companies who have been developing enterprise-scale component-based applications since 1996 in a variety of vertical domains, from telecoms to transportation, and finance to manufacturing. At the time of writing, the CBD CAB has around one hundred member companies.

These companies have helped to separate what works in practice and has genuine, practical added value from what sounds good but is impractical on a real project. They've kept our feet firmly on the ground.

What works in practice is often a function of how well a particular process or technique is supported by application development tools. And it has to be said, most UML tools don't do a great job of supporting component-based development. We avoid references to specific tools in this book since we want it to have a broad appeal, and we try to keep as close to standard UML as we can, defining a relatively small set of extensions. But clearly, the better your tool of choice supports these concepts and processes, the more practical you will find them.

Acknowledgments

As detailed earlier, we acknowledge the work of others that has provided the source for many of the ideas that we've brought together here.

We condensed all of these ideas into a cohesive whole during 1999, while we were both working at Sterling Software's Chertsey Lab in England. We would like to thank all the members of that team for their support and help. In particular, we would like to acknowledge the contribution of John Dodd, with whom we spent many hours debating the details of particular approaches and considering the practicability of some of the techniques.

The prize for keeping us practical must go to the Sterling Software CBD CAB.

Paul Harmon from the Cutter Consortium provided useful independent analysis of our CBD approach and our concept models.

Our formal reviewers provided timely, insightful, and constructive feedback, as well as encouragement that we were saying something useful and new. We would like to thank Paul Allen; John Dodd; Chris Lamela, IntellectMarket, Inc.; Pete McBreen; and Alan Cameron Wills, TriReme International Ltd.

Additional helpful comments and support came from Laura Hill, Bruce Anderson, and Richard Mitchell. Thanks also to James Noble for suggesting the title.

Thanks to Kristin Erickson at Addison-Wesley for her enthusiasm and support throughout, and to the team there for processing the book on a tight schedule.

John Cheesman
Surrey, England
johnc@componentsource.com

John Daniels
London, England
john@syntropy.co.uk

Chapter 1

Component Systems

C omponents aren't rocket science. Try explaining the basic principles of component-based development to someone not involved in the information technology (IT) industry and they're likely to be somewhat underwhelmed. Despite this apparent simplicity, there seems to be widespread misunderstanding and confusion about the concepts that underlie components and about what makes them special. In this chapter we take a tour around some of the major topics that distinguish component systems from systems built using other approaches. We also establish some terminology and concepts, and set out our approach to structuring component systems. The goal is to get acquainted with the basic mindset needed so that you are well armed before we plunge into the Unified Modeling Language (UML) and our case study.

1.1 Component Goals

Component systems adhere to the principle of divide and conquer for managing complexity—break a large problem down into smaller pieces and solve those smaller pieces, then build up more elaborate solutions from simpler foundations. Easy. To many this sounds like the structured methods that have been followed for years, so what's different?

The principal difference is that components follow the object principle of combining functions and related data into a single unit. Traditional structured approaches have tended to focus mainly on functional decomposition and have maintained a strong distinction between data and function.

1

There's one thing that's worth getting clear early on—what major challenge is the component approach to system development addressing? For us that challenge is managing change. This means building for change in the first place by placing primary emphasis during architecture and design on the dependencies between the components, and the management of those dependencies. The purpose of the individual components is clearly important but is in many ways a secondary concern.

This may surprise some people. Many think the primary objective of components is reuse. They want to design something once and use it over and over again in different contexts, thereby realizing large productivity gains, taking advantage of best-in-class solutions, the consequent improved quality, and so forth. These are admirable objectives, but the main driver today is that things keep changing, and often—as with business-to-business electronic commerce—there is no longer any hope that centralized control can be exerted. In such an environment one of the primary objectives of a component is that it must be easily replaceable—either by a completely different implementation of the same functions or by an upgraded version of the current implementation. This places the emphasis on the architecture of the system, on being able to manage the total system, as its various components evolve and its requirements change, rather than seeking to ensure that individual components are reusable by multiple component systems.

We're focusing on the whole, rather than the parts.

1.2   Component Principles

Components, as found in the component technologies we are considering here, are units of software structured according to some specific principles. The fundamental principles they adhere to are actually the fundamental principles that underpin object technology:

1. **Unification of data and function:** A software object consists of data values (or state) and the functions that process those data. This natural colocation of dependencies between function and data improves cohesion.

2. **Encapsulation:** The client[1] of a software object is insulated from how that software object's data is stored or how its functions are implemented. We say that the client depends on the object specification, but not its implementation. This is a very important separation of concerns and is key to managing dependencies between software and reducing coupling.

3. **Identity:** Each software object has a unique identity, regardless of state.

Components extend these object principles by elaborating the notion of an object specification with an explicit representation of specification dependency called an *interface*. This is an important level of indirection between the client of an object and the capabilities of that object. The specification of the total capabilities of an object may be split across several interfaces.

To summarize: Component-based development is different from previous approaches in its separation of component specification from implementation, and in the division of component specifications into interfaces.

Splitting component specifications into one or more interfaces means that the intercomponent dependencies can be restricted to individual interfaces, rather than encompass the whole component specification. This reduces the impact of change because one consumed component may replace another even if it has a different specification, as long as its specification includes the same interfaces the consuming components require.

These characteristics allow a component to be upgraded or replaced with minimal impact on the clients of that component.

Figure 1.1 shows an existing component being replaced by a new one. An existing client will use established interfaces (characterized by IX) and will be unaffected—new components can be plugged in to existing clients if they offer the old interfaces. They may also provide new functionality (IX+) for new clients.

Clients may also be flexible in their requirements of components. They may require certain interfaces as a minimum, but will leverage additional or newer interfaces if they are available.

---

1. *Client* here means consuming or calling software.

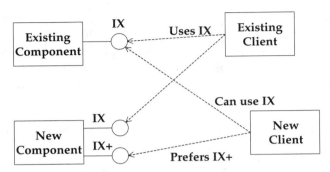

Figure 1.1   Interface dependency supports component replacement

1.3   Component Forms

So, what exactly is a component? This is actually a surprisingly difficult question to answer simply, even when you restrict your definition of components to current technologies, because the word *component* is used informally to mean a variety of things, each with apparent equal validity.

A better question, and one we *can* answer simply, is, What features does a component have and how does our view of it change during a project life cycle? From requirements and specification, through design and provisioning, to assembly, deployment, and runtime, the characteristics we want from a component vary. We can identify a number of component forms, each form reflecting some aspect of a component during the development life cycle.

So, in fact, we won't define component at all; instead we define the many forms a component can take.

- Being able to assemble applications from components means that components must conform to some sort of environment standard—they form part of a component kit. Just like buying an off-the-shelf part in any other domain (such as computer hardware, automobiles, or washing machines) a component will only plug in if it conforms to some laid down set of base standards. So, the shape of the plug-in piece is important. Let's call this the **Component Standard**. Enterprise JavaBeans (EJB) and Microsoft's COM+ are examples of such standards. Some large organizations have defined their own. Provided you have one and it meets your needs it doesn't much matter what it is, but we claim that it is meaningless to talk about components unless you have a standard—or possibly more than one—in mind.

- When you go looking for a component to plug in, having the right shape plug is certainly a good start, but knowing what that part does is pretty important too. Consider the fuse that's probably sitting in the power supply of your computer: It's no use buying a 5-amp fuse when you need a 15-amp fuse. They both slot in nicely, but one will blow when it shouldn't, or conversely one won't blow when it should. So, the specification of what a component does must also be part of a valid definition—we need a clear **Component Specification**.

- A major part of a component specification is the definition of **Component Interfaces**, or just **Interface** for short.

- The specification of the component is more important, from an assembly perspective, than the way that specification is realized or implemented. It should be possible to replace one component with another (of an equivalent specification) without affecting the assembly. For example, you may want to be able to replace one 15-amp fuse with another from a different manufacturer. What matters from an assembly point of view is the interdependency between the parts, not the way those parts work. The clear separation of component specification from **Component Implementation** is therefore another important characteristic of a component. The assembly itself should only depend on the specification. If there is any dependency on the implementation then the ability to replace that piece easily will be lost.

The lack of dependency on implementation means that software components can be implemented in any programming language using any data storage mechanism. In particular, this means that existing software, which may not initially meet all the requirements of a component, can be updated, sometimes very simply, so that it conforms to the component standard and becomes a valid component.

- It is the component implementations that are deployed onto machines. Each time we install a component implementation we create an **Installed Component** (i.e., an installed version of the component, known to the environment).

- We also need to consider the existence of state or content of the component at runtime. While the software services provided by a component are important, so is the information managed by that component. When replacing a component it is not usually enough to substitute equivalent services—the information managed must also be equivalent. Imagine replacing a component managing millions of customers to find that the new component provided equivalent customer management services but had no knowledge of the customers! Similarly, we might want to manage European and U.S. customers separately, using two different instances of the same component. Since we are now referring to services and state together, a key object principle, we call each instance created from an installed component a **Component Object**. It is these component objects that have an identity. Only component objects can actually *do* anything.

It would be useful if UML directly supported all these distinctions about components, but unfortunately it doesn't. In Chapter 3 we explain how we can adapt UML for use in modeling components.

We've introduced quite a number of important distinctions that are needed when modeling components. These are summarized in Figure 1.2 and Table 1.1.

1.3.1   Example: Microsoft Word

As an example, consider Microsoft Word and its components. Word comprises many components but two of the most obvious are those representing the application itself and the documents you open or create. Referring to Figure 1.3, we assume that back at Microsoft HQ there exist specifications of these two components, but these aren't supplied on the CD. Instead we get an executable file called winword.exe that packages the Component Implementations. These are implementations specific to the Component Standard we are using, for example COM.

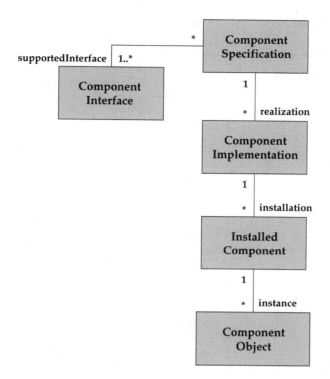

Figure 1.2 Component forms

Simplifying somewhat, installing Word involves copying the physical file winword.exe into a known location and registering its contents with the runtime environment (in this case COM). This creates two Installed Components—components known to COM. Running the Word application initially creates two Component Objects: one representing the application object itself, which acts as a frame, and another as a default new document object. Further document objects can be created using the File/New command on the application object.

1.3.2　What a Component Isn't

We hope you've followed the logic so far. But to rule out any possible confusion we'll take a moment to explain some things that a component isn't.

Table 1.1 Component form descriptions

Component Form	Description
Component Specification	The specification of a unit of software that describes the behavior of a set of Component Objects and defines a unit of implementation. *Behavior* is defined as a set of Interfaces. A Component Specification is realized as a Component Implementation.
Component Interface	A definition of a set of behaviors that can be offered by a Component Object.
Component Implementation	A realization of a Component Specification, which is independently deployable. This means it can be installed and replaced independently of other components. It does not mean that it is independent of other components—it may have many dependencies. It does not necessarily mean that it is a single physical item, such as a single file.
Installed Component	An installed (or deployed) copy of a Component Implementation. A Component Implementation is deployed by registering it with the runtime environment. This enables the runtime environment to identify the Installed Component to use when creating an instance of the component, or when running one of its operations.
Component Object	An instance of an Installed Component. A runtime concept. An object with its own data and a unique identity. The thing that performs the implemented behavior. An Installed Component may have multiple Component Objects (which require explicit identification) or a single one (which may be implicit).

A component isn't an object, not in the sense of simply being an object in a Java or C++ program. It's true that at runtime we have Component Objects that exhibit most of the characteristics of programming language objects, but they exist in the context of a Component Standard, such as provided by an EJB server. Component Objects can only exist in such a context.

A component isn't a service, although one of the things you can do with components is build **Service-Based Architectures**, where each Component Object provides a specific function, using specific data. But components can equally well be used to abstract data, as you will see later in this book.

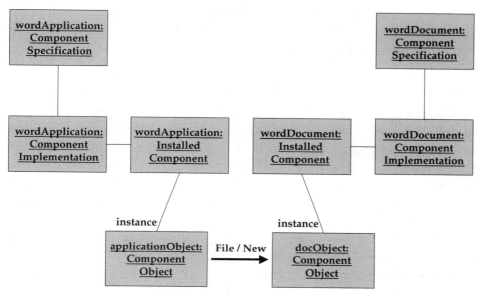

Figure 1.3　Microsoft Word

1.4　Component and System Architectures

Architecture is one of those words that has lost some of its meaning over time. There are so many types of architecture in common usage we need first to define what we mean by the term. Here we are going to describe **System Architectures** and **Component Architectures**.

We define system architecture to be

> *the structure of the pieces that make up a complete software installation, including the responsibilities of these pieces, their interconnection, and possibly even the appropriate technology.*

We define a component architecture as

> *a set of application-level software components, their structural relationships, and their behavioral dependencies.*

So we are following the trend of using architecture to mean the overall structure of a system or family of systems. Whatever word you choose for this, it is undeniably important to understand the big picture: what pieces you've got, how they fit together, and what the impact of change might be. That is the value of architecture.

1.4.1   System Architectures

Our aim in this book is to provide advice, guidance, and examples for modeling enterprise-scale component systems. This means we're considering N-tier distributed architectures, linking corporate databases, off-the-shelf packages, and legacy systems, through business-process-specific application software to web-based user interfaces. A typical system architecture for the kinds of systems we have in mind is shown in Figure 1.4.

Understanding the system architecture is important because it tells us the overall shape of the final system and explains how we will use various technologies to assemble the system we need.

Architecture Layers

We want to use components for different purposes and to keep different concerns separate. Our general approach is to identify different layers into which

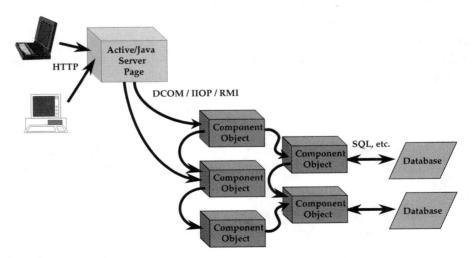

Figure 1.4   Typical system architecture

components can fit (see Figure 1.5). This is useful because it allows us to reason about the purpose of each software unit we put into the application.

The layers are as follows:

- **User interface**—the presentation of information to the users and the capture of their inputs. External systems can be users, too. Although there might be things called components in this layer (e.g., user interface widgets), they won't be the kind of components we're considering in this book.

- **User dialog**—management of the user's dialog in a session. Once again, we aren't, in this book, dealing with components in this layer.

- **System services**—the external representation of the system, providing access to the services of the system. This layer acts as a facade for the layer below, providing a context within which the more general business services are used to meet the needs of this particular system.

- **Business services**—the implementation of core business information, rules, and transformations. These are often reused across several systems.

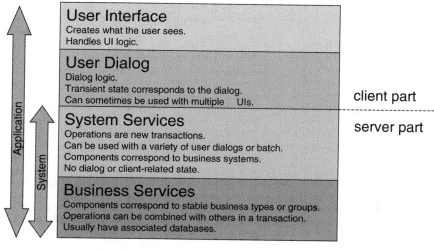

Figure 1.5   Architectural layers

We consider the bottom two layers to form the **System,** which we define to be user interface (UI) independent. When a UI is connected to the system we have an **Application**. Many different UIs may be connected simultaneously to a single system. Figure 1.6 shows an example of the component objects we might find in the system layers, using the specific technology of the Java 2 Enterprise Edition.

We aren't making hard and fast rules about the use of these layers. For example, we don't insist that communication is always between adjacent layers. A common case is when the user dialog layer directly accesses the business services layer. In some systems the system services layer might be completely empty, implying that the underlying business service components require no management to allow them to function in the context of this system. At the other extreme, we might instigate a rule that all access to the business service component objects is always via a single system service component object (sometimes called a "radial architecture") because we want to keep the lower-level component objects isolated, hopefully improving the interchangeability and reuse potential of each component.

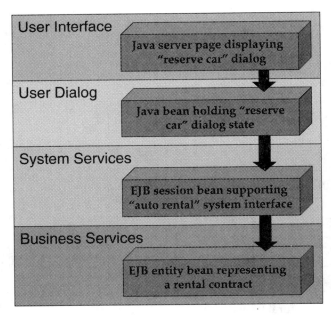

Figure 1.6   Example components in the layers

1.4.2 Component Architectures

Components of some form or another might be found in all four layers of the system architecture. However, this book is concerned with the server parts of the application, so we will focus on modeling the components that live in the system services and business services layers.

We said before that a **Component Architecture** is a set of application-level software components, their structural relationships, and their behavioral dependencies. This is a logical definition and is independent of the technology level on which it will be deployed. A component architecture may apply to a single application or to a wider context, such as a set of applications serving a particular business process area. Creating this logical view of the components allows us to understand how tightly or loosely coupled our system is, and to reason about the effects of modifying or replacing a component.

By structural relationships we mean associations and inheritance between component specifications and component interfaces, and composition relationships between components. By behavioral dependencies we mean dependency relationships between components and other components, between components and interfaces, and between interfaces (see Figure 1.7).[2]

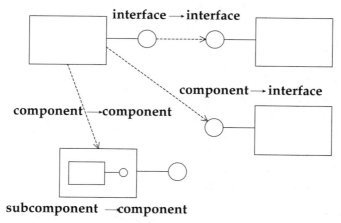

Figure 1.7 Dependencies in component architectures

---

2. Subcomponents are discussed in Chapter 8.

Component Specification Architectures

It is possible to create component architectures that focus on either component specifications, component implementations, or component objects. A **Component Specification Architecture** diagram contains only component specifications and interfaces. All dependencies take the form of an interface or a component specification depending on an interface. The important rule for specification architectures is this:

> *Any dependency emanating from a component specification is part of the definition of that component specification and must be adhered to by all implementations.*

The dependency acts as a constraint on all implementations of the specification: Any implementation must exhibit this dependency. Typically the dependencies in a component specification architecture are derivable from more detailed parts of the specification, such as interaction diagrams.

Do we really need to specify, at an architectural level, all these dependencies? Can't we leave many of the decisions to the component designers? In an isolated development project many of the component dependencies may be left as a design decision, but for larger-scale, enterprise-wide application development, the component specification architecture is a critical aspect of the wider IT architecture. It is not up to individual application development teams to pick and choose which components they wish to reuse—it is often an architectural constraint placed on them by a centralized architecture team.

By being explicit about the specification dependencies, a component specification architecture can be used as a mechanism for ensuring that broader standards, policies, and approaches are followed. For example, an individual application may find the performance overhead of an accounting component unnecessary. But if its use is made standard policy by enforcing the rule that every component must use its services, then broader benefits can follow, such as standardized accounting or reporting across all applications.

Component Implementation Architectures

The **Component Implementation Architecture** shows the actual dependencies that exist between particular component implementations. These will be the union of the dependencies that are specified and those introduced by the component realizers: Component implementations may interact with components not mentioned in the specification, and they may have additional interactions with components that are mentioned.

Component Object Architectures

We hear a lot about component reuse in the press. This may be a straight-forward goal for stateless components, but for stateful components it is also important to understand, and be precise about, which component objects are being used.

Consider the situation where a component specification architecture defines that both the order manager component and the stock control component must use the product manager component (see Figure 1.8).

Although the intent, and even the impression, may be that there is a single set of product information accessed by the two calling components, the model does not state that this must be the case. To be precise we need to use a **Component Object Architecture**, specifying the instances of components that will be accessed.

In Figure 1.9, two alternative component object architectures are shown, each conforming to the component specification architecture in Figure 1.8. In Figure 1.9(a) the order manager and the stock control component objects share a common product manager component object. In Figure 1.9(b) each has its own instance of the product manager component and manages a distinct set of product information.

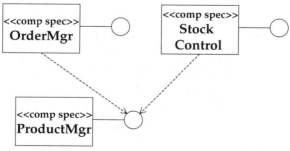

Figure 1.8   Component specification architecture

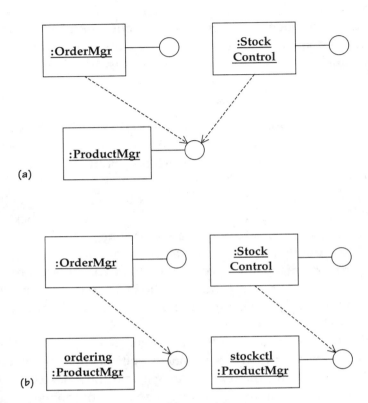

Figure 1.9   Alternative component object architectures

1.5   Specifying Contracts

Designing good component-based software can be seen, at the macro-scopic or architectural level, as a dependency management problem. We are seeking to ensure that pieces of software, developed at different times by different people, possibly from different organizations, can work together successfully. How can we do this?

Well, software development is a relatively new discipline in the grand scheme of things. Software engineers haven't had long to work it all out, so let's draw on the experience of other human endeavors that have analo-gous issues and that have stood the test of time. We might learn something useful. If we think of a component as a piece of software that provides some sort of service, and requires services of others, we can usefully make an analogy between components and companies.

Companies are entities that provide services to their customers (which may be other companies, organizations, or individuals) and that often depend on the services of other companies. How do companies manage their relationships in the real world? They do it through contracts. A contract is a formal agreement between two or more parties. It describes (or specifies) the detail of the agreement in an unambiguous form. This involves stating the responsibilities or obligations of each party—what each party will do provided the other parties do what they say they will do. It does not state how they will do it, simply that they will. Importantly, it also states what will happen if the parties do not do what they say—if they fail to provide the agreed service.

The analogous **Design by Contract** has proved very useful in software design. It was developed extensively in the object-oriented domain by Bertrand Meyer [Meyer00] and applied to the component world by Catalysis [D'Souza99]. Building on this work, we can apply design by contract to UML and today's component technologies.

We distinguish two different types of contract:

1. **Usage**—the contract between a component object's interface and its clients

2. **Realization**—the contract between a component specification and its implementation

These different aspects are shown in Figure 1.10.

It's important to distinguish these contracts because they correspond to the roles often played in the development of large component systems: The people who build components are often not the same people who use them. The contents and purpose of the contracts are really quite different.

The specification of a component is composed of many parts, not all of them relevant to the client. Defining which interfaces the component must offer is just part of the whole component specification. The interface defines everything the client needs to know, but no more than that. An interface doesn't, for example, specify how implementations of this interface must interact with other components to fulfil their responsibilities; that is defined in the component specification itself. The interface specification may imply

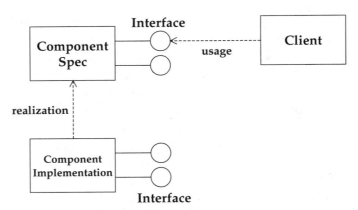

Figure 1.10   Different types of contracts

interactions but it does not specify how they happen. Other parts of the component specification do this.

The primary reason for keeping these things separate is to facilitate change: A change to the realization constraints does not constitute a change to the usage contract, and hence does not affect clients. This is important because it gives us the ability to change specifications that affect realization without having to revalidate all client usage.

1.5.1   Usage Contracts

A **Usage Contract** (see Figure 1.11) describes the relationship between a component object's interface and a client, and is specified in the form of an interface. The client is left unspecified because we can't predict who will use an interface in the future. The specification of an interface includes the following:

- **Operations**—a list of operations that the interface provides, including their signatures and definitions

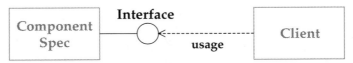

Figure 1.11   Usage contract

- **Information model**—the abstract definition of any information or state that is retained between client requests by an object supporting the interface, and any constraints on that information

Each operation is treated as a fine-grained contract in its own right. It defines its inputs, its outputs, the relationship between them, and the conditions under which they apply. The reason for grouping operations into larger-grained contractual units (i.e., interfaces) is because their pragmatic usage needs the existence of other operations and because they are rarely used independently of those other operations.

As well as a signature, each operation is defined by the following:

- **Precondition**—a definition of the situations under which the post-condition will apply
- **Postcondition**—a description of the effects of that operation on its parameters and the information model

The onus is on the client to ensure that the precondition of an operation is true before making a call. By agreeing to the contract, it accepts that if the precondition isn't met the expected behavior might not happen. For its part the supplier promises to satisfy the postcondition if the precondition was met. It's important to understand that if the precondition isn't met, the result of the operation is undefined—anything could happen.

Consider an order management application (see Table 1.2) with an interface IOrder defining the capabilities of an individual Order, with an operation createOrderLine( ) which takes as input a product-type identifier and a quantity. Here's the deal: The client ensures that the type of product being ordered is valid and that at least one is being ordered, while the supplier (the object supporting IOrder) makes sure an order line is created.

Using pre- and postconditions doesn't automatically imply a high degree of precision, but precise specifications are very valuable in defining components

Table 1.2 Order line creation contract

Party	Responsibility
Client	Product type exists and quantity > 0
IOrder	Order line created

that can be replaced painlessly. Typically, much of the work involved in specifying interfaces centers around making the pre- and postconditions precise, often using a formal language. We explain this more fully in Chapter 7.

1.5.2 Realization Contracts

A usage contract is a runtime contract, but a **Realization Contract** is a designtime contract. It is a contract between a component specification and a component implementation, and must be adhered to by the person who is creating the implementation: the realizer. The realization contract is embodied in the component specification itself (see Figure 1.12).

While an interface defines a set of behavior, a component specification defines an implementation and deployment boundary. By specifying a set of interfaces that must be supported, a component specification defines the total sum of capabilities of any object created at runtime from the implementation. The component specification can also define how the implementation must interact with other components. We may want to instruct any implementer of the component specification that he or she must include particular interactions with other components as part of the implementation of operations. Knowledge of such interactions does not form part of the interface specification and so cannot be directly known by the client. We define these interaction constraints either procedurally using collaboration diagrams, or declaratively using constraints between the information models of the supported and used interfaces.

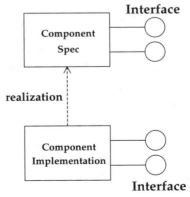

Figure 1.12   Realizing a component specification

Finally, a component specification can specify how one supported interface must correspond to another. As noted, an interface specification contains an information model: an abstract model of the information retained by the component between operations. When a component supports two or more interfaces, elements in that information model of one interface often correspond directly to elements in the information models of other supported interfaces, and must always have the same value. Similarly, an element in the information model of a supported interface may correspond to an element in a used interface. We specify such constraints between interface information models as part of the component specification.

All this information, together with the specifications of the supported interfaces, constitutes the realization contract.

1.5.3 Interfaces versus Component Specifications

Although at first sight it may not be apparent why we need both interface and component specification as separate concepts, they perform quite distinct functions. The component specification forms the contract with the component realizer, assembler, and tester. A component specification scopes the implementation unit, defines the encapsulation boundary, and consequently determines the granularity of replaceability in the system. The interface forms the contract with the component client. It tells the client what to expect. Table 1.3 summarizes the differences between an interface and a component specification.

Table 1.3 Interface versus component specification

Interface	Component Specification
A list of operations	A list of supported interfaces
Defines an underlying logical information model	Defines the relationships between the information models of different interfaces
Represents the contract with the client	Represents the contract with the implementer
Specifies how operations affect or rely on the information model	Defines the implementation and runtime unit
Describes local effects only	Specifies how operations must be implemented in terms of usage of other interfaces

1.6   Model Levels

In this book we talk a lot about models, mostly using UML as our modeling language. We need to be clear on the purpose of these models.

Any model of something is a perspective or view—it includes and emphasizes some things and excludes others. That's the value of a model. For example, a map of a country could highlight political boundaries, geography, geology, transport, industry, population, economics, ecology, and so on. If you draw a map for someone and you want them to understand it, they'd better know what all the lines mean and what the perspective is. That's what the map key is for. It's the same with models in the software domain. How can we ensure that two people both understand the meaning of a box and line diagram in the same way?

UML provides a standard language that can be used in many ways. In particular, it is useful to distinguish three quite different semantic levels of model that are frequently drawn using UML [Cook94] [Fowler99]:

1. **Conceptual models**—software-independent models that identify the concepts in the domain being studied

2. **Specification models**—software-specific models that define the specification of the software, not its implementation details; models of the "outsides" of components

3. **Implementation models**—models that detail the implementation design of the software; models of the "insides" of components

In fact UML contains elements that correspond to different levels of model. For example, the class concept has stereotypes for «type» and «implementationClass»; but more about that in Chapter 3.

Since we're interested in how to model components and their dependencies, we'll be dealing mainly with specification models—the outsides of components. We'll be showing how UML can be applied to model these outsides in a precise manner. We won't concern ourselves with the insides of components (their internal design and implementation) other than their implementation dependencies on other components. A component may be implemented in any language, from COBOL to Java. That's one of the useful things about them.

What's more, we'll be focusing on applying UML to models of software applications, not to business or technology models. Application models focus on the structure of an application and usually exclude considerations of the underlying technology on which that application is based. For example, an application model may describe dependencies between a product management component, an order management component, and a billing component, but not show what distributed component standard they conform to or what language they are implemented in.

1.7   Summary

This book is concerned with specification of business systems.

Components adopt object principles: unification of data and function, encapsulation, and identity. Components extend these principles by strengthening the role of the interface and by adding a separate notion of component specification. Components must conform to a component standard.

The systems we are targeting with this book can be structured into four layers:

- User interface
- User dialog
- System services
- Business services

These layers and the dependencies between them constitute a system architecture.

A component architecture is concerned with the structure and dependencies between components in the system services and business services layers. The component specification architecture describes the constraints on the implementation and assembly of components to form the system. The component implementation architecture describes the actual dependencies between specific component implementations.

The component object architecture describes the runtime situation: what instances of components there are and the dependencies between these instances.

The component specification defines what is to be built and what units will exist at runtime. The component specification defines the set of interfaces supported and any constraints on how they are to be implemented. It is the contract between the specifier and the realizer: the realization contract.

An interface specifies the operations it contains. Each operation specification is a contract between the invoker and the component providing the operation. Interfaces are usage contracts.

Chapter 2

The Development Process

A ll software development projects follow two distinct processes at the same time. The **Management Process** schedules work, plans deliveries, allocates resources, and monitors progress. The **Development Process** creates working software from requirements. Assuming you have these processes written down, you would consult your management process guide if you wanted help with setting milestones and your development process guide if you wanted help with allocating operations to interfaces.

The software process literature contains examples of methods that include either or both of these processes. For example, Dynamic Systems Development Method (DSDM) is a management process [DSDM], Catalysis is mostly a development process [D'Souza99], and the Rational Unified Process (RUP) [Jacobson99] covers both.

Although it hasn't always been this way, today the development process has to be subservient to the management process. This is because the management process controls project risk, and risk control is rightly viewed as paramount, even if the development process is compromised as a result. The favored management process nowadays is one based on evolution, where the software is delivered over a number of development iterations, each refining and building on the one before [Gilb88, GilbWeb]. The development process has to fit with that, so it isn't possible to specify everything, then design everything, then code everything, and so on, even if you wanted to.

Nevertheless, when we describe the development process we do so without taking into account the constraints of the management process. We do this because we want the development process to be usable with a variety of management processes. It also helps to make the development process understandable. We revisit the effects of the management process after we have explained the development process.

As you might have guessed from the title of this chapter, we explain our preferred development process here and throughout the rest of the book, but we do not cover the details of the various possible management processes.

2.1 Workflows

Figure 2.1 shows the overall development process. The boxes represent **Workflows**, as found in RUP. In his book on RUP, Philippe Kruchten defines a workflow as "a sequence of activities that produces a result of observable value" [Kruchten99]. The thin arrows represent the flow of **Artifacts**—deliverables that carry information between workflows. Comparing the workflows of Figure 2.1 to those found in RUP, the requirements, test, and deployment workflows correspond directly to those with the same names in RUP and are not discussed further in this book, with the exception of some minor elaboration of the requirements workflow. The specification, provisioning, and assembly workflows replace RUP's analysis and design and implementation workflows, and they define the scope of this book (see Figure 2.2).

Our primary concern is the specification workflow. Chapter 4 covers just those aspects of the requirements workflow that we need to generate inputs for specification. The specification workflow is divided into three sections: component identification, component interaction, and component specification (Chapters 5, 6, and 7). Chapter 8 covers sufficient parts of the provisioning and assembly workflows to give you at least a taste of implementation.

The specification workflow takes as its input from requirements a use case model and a business concept model. It also uses information about existing software assets, such as legacy systems, packages, and databases,

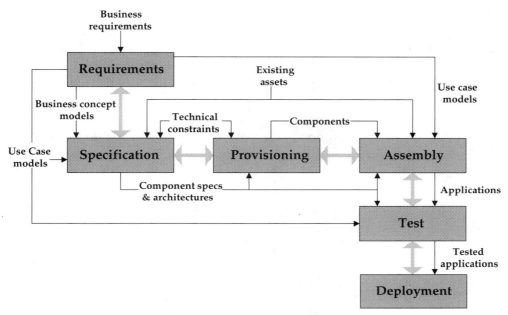

Figure 2.1   The workflows in the overall development process

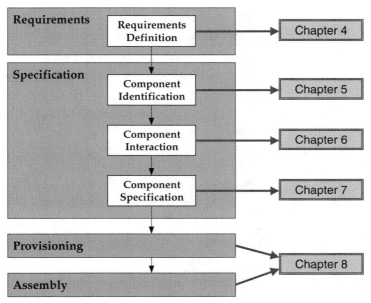

Figure 2.2   Workflow mappings to chapters

and technical constraints, such as use of particular architectures or tools. It generates a set of component specifications and a component architecture. The component specifications include the interface specifications they support or depend on, and the component architecture shows how the components interact with each other.

These outputs are used in the provisioning workflow to determine what components to build or buy, in the assembly workflow to guide the correct integration of components, and in the test workflow as an input to test scripts.

The provisioning workflow ensures that the necessary components are made available, either by building them from scratch, buying them from a third party, or reusing, integrating, mining, or otherwise modifying an existing component or other software. The provisioning workflow also includes unit testing the component prior to assembly.

The assembly workflow takes all the components and puts them together with existing software assets and a suitable user interface to form an application that meets the business need.

2.2 The Impact of the Management Process

2.2.1 The Evolution of Software Processes

The optimal development process—assuming an ideal, stable, and unchanging world—is one that gathers complete requirements, specifies completely a system to meet the requirements, designs all the software pieces, implements and integrates them, and tests the result. This is optimal, at least in theory, because doing all the design up front means you won't have to change the software once it has been written, and changing software has traditionally been expensive. But the risks inherent in this kind of waterfall process are well known, so the truly optimal management process, with risk management at its heart, takes a quite different tack. It insists that partial systems are delivered early and built incrementally. It assumes that requirements will change or, at best, are incompletely understood. It acknowledges that software might have to be changed as the truth behind the requirements emerges but accepts that as a price worth paying.

Early software methods often had a management process that followed, and was subservient to, the development process. Although such methods were fine for designing software, they were poor at controlling risks, with inevitable results. The reaction to the failure of these methods was the rise of methods that focused only or mainly on the management process, methods with a rapid application development (RAD) style. The predictable consequence was the creation of systems that were delivered on time but with very poor structure, making them difficult and expensive to change and extend. In turn, the reaction to RAD has been the rise of "architecture" as a rallying word for the reintroduction of sound design practices. Recent methods such as RUP attempt to achieve balance between the processes by setting out a full development process that lives within a rigid time-boxed management structure.

An interesting recent development has been the assertion by some leaders in the object technology community that by using modern software tools and techniques—especially planned refactoring of working software to improve its structure—the cost of changing software can be greatly reduced. They propose a method, called eXtreme Programming (XP), that adopts a highly iterative style and requires extensive changes to software already built and tested [Beck99]. XP relies on the belief that the cost of change can be made so low that an iterative and incremental development process, aligned completely with the iterative management process, can be as efficient as a linear one. If that is true, the two processes are no longer in tension.

2.2.2   Accommodating Change

Although the development process outlined here can be used with any management process, we assume you will be using a management process based on evolutionary delivery, and such processes require change to the software at each iteration.[1] As you will recall from Chapter 1, we think the major motivation for using a component approach is to manage change better. So there is a natural fit between components and evolutionary delivery.

---

1. Evolutionary delivery really combines iterative and incremental techniques: Each cycle of development both refines the existing artifacts and produces new ones.

Every iteration typically involves activities from all the workflows in the development process. The activities improve and extend the artifacts produced in the last iteration.

Figure 2.3 illustrates the evolution of artifacts during a project comprising five iterations. The first iteration concentrated on the requirements workflow, so the business concept model and use case model were substantially completed. But a small amount of work was done, even on the first iteration, in the specification, provisioning, and other workflows to demonstrate technical feasibility, as required for risk management. Each successive iteration has a different focus, but, even in the fourth iteration, for example, it may be necessary to revisit the requirements workflow use case model.

Actually, the whole notion of completion is highly suspect. Projects end when we have "done enough" —that is, when we decide that no more money should be spent on these artifacts, either because they meet the business need well enough or because it looks as though they never will. Of course, we hope that the artifacts produced by successful projects will have a long and glorious life. That life will inevitably involve changes, so it is important to design components to be amenable to both short- and long-term change.

But don't get carried away. It's extremely unlikely you will be able to predict the changes required for a component over its lifetime, and attempts explicitly to design-in multiple axes of change are likely to be expensive mistakes. However, the power of encapsulation means we can change pretty much anything about a component's implementation with only limited impact on the whole system. And factoring a component's capabilities into multiple interfaces reduces the impact of interface

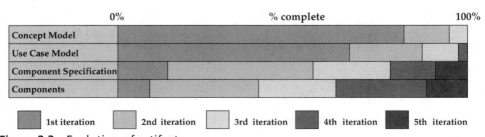

Figure 2.3 Evolution of artifacts

changes. So simply by following component principles you'll get a powerful ability to react to change. When we say that components help with change we mean that their inherent characteristics limit the effects of change, not that they eliminate the need for change itself.

2.3   Workflow Artifacts

The requirements and specification workflows are responsible for producing a number of model artifacts. The main requirements artifacts we'll be dealing with are the **Business Concept Model** and the **Use Case Model**. In specification we'll be producing the **Business Type Model, Interface Specifications, Component Specifications,** and **Component Architecture.**

We've found it helpful to organize our model elements into a package structure that reflects these artifacts (see Figure 2.4).[2] Subsequent chapters elaborate on this structure as we explain how UML is applied to model each of the artifacts, and as we develop the case study.

The business concept model is a conceptual model of the business domain that needs to be understood and agreed. Its main purpose is to create a common vocabulary among the business people involved with the project. For example, if "customer" means three different things within the business, you need to get this cleared up as early as possible so that everyone is working to the same set of terms with agreed meanings.

A use case is a way of specifying certain aspects of the functional requirements of the system. It describes interactions between a user (or other external actor) and the system, and therefore helps to define what we call the system boundary. The use case model is the set of use cases you consider to be representative of the total functional requirements. You might start with the key ones, then add others later.

The business type model is an intermediate specification artifact and not an output of the specification workflow. Its purpose is to formalize the

---

2. As part of the management process you may wish vary from this, for example to keep multiple versions of certain artifacts and to retain intermediate refinement states, but these aspects are not shown.

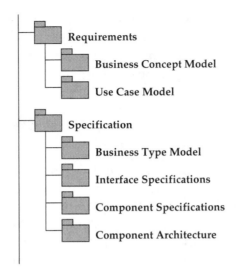

Figure 2.4   Top-level organization of workflow artifacts

business concept model to define the system's knowledge of the outside world. This model is the basis for initial interface identification. While the business concept model describes the business domain as the business people understand it, the business type model captures exactly those aspects and rules of the business domain that the system knows about. The business concept model may be imprecise, but the business type model must be precise.

The interface specifications artifact is a set of individual interface specifications. Each interface specification is a contract with a client of a component object. Each interface specification defines the details of its contract in terms of the operations it provides, what their signatures are, what effects they have on the parameters of the operations and the state of the component object, and under what conditions these effects are guaranteed. This is where most of the detailed system behavior decisions are pinned down.

The component specifications artifact is a set of individual component specifications. Each component specification is defined in terms of interface specifications and constraints. A component specification defines the interfaces it supports and how their specifications correspond to each other. It also includes the interfaces it uses or consumes. While an interface specification represents the contract with the client, the component specification pulls these disparate client contracts together to define a single realization contract. This is where the building blocks of the system are defined.

The component architecture describes how the component specifications fit together in a given configuration. It binds the interface dependencies of the individual component specifications into component dependencies and describes how the component objects interact with each other. The architecture shows how the building blocks fit together to form a system that meets the requirements.

In Chapter 3 we explain how we model these artifacts in UML.

2.4 The Specification Workflow

The specification workflow is rather tricky to explain because explanations tend to be sequential, whereas the workflow tasks are highly iterative. The various workflow artifacts have clear dependencies, but their development is incremental, with additions and modifications at every stage. We have attempted to summarize the workflow tasks into the three stages: component identification, component interaction, and component specification (see Figure 2.5). For the most part you can take the word "component" here to be shorthand for "component and interface."

Note also that since we are staying management-process neutral, we haven't attempted to characterize the degree of completeness, or other quality criteria, of these workflow artifacts. The management process phases specify those.

2.4.1 Component Identification

The component identification stage takes as input the business concept model and the use case model from the requirements workflow. It assumes an application layering that includes a separation of system components and business components, as discussed in Chapter 1. Its goal is to identify an initial set of business interfaces for the business components and an initial set of system interfaces for the system components, and to pull these together into an initial component architecture. The business type model is an intermediate artifact from which the initial business interfaces are

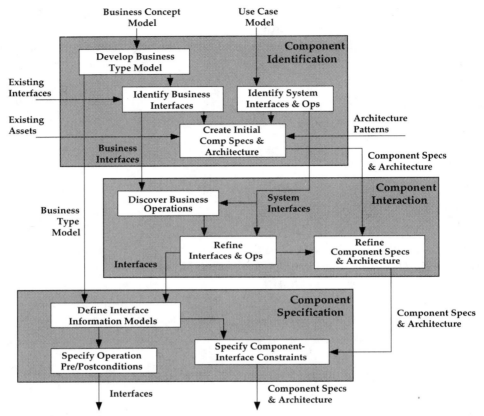

Figure 2.5   The three stages of the specification workflow

formed. It is also used later, in the component specification stage, as the raw material for the development of interface information models.

Any existing components or other software assets need to be taken into account too, as well as any architecture patterns you plan to use. At this stage it's fairly broad-brush stuff, intended to set out the component and interface landscape for subsequent refinement.

In addition to identifying system interfaces, the identification stage also makes a first cut at the operations that need to be supported by the system. These are identified by name, but signatures and others details are added at a later stage. The system operations required are derived by examining the steps in the different use cases and deciding what the system's responsibilities are.

2.4.2   Component Interaction

The component interaction stage examines how each of the system operations will be achieved using the component architecture. It uses interaction models to discover operations on the business interfaces. As more interactions are considered, common operations and patterns of usage emerge that can be factored out and reused. Responsibility choices become clearer and operations are moved from one interface to another. Alternative groupings of interfaces into components can be investigated. This is the time to think through the management of references between component objects so that dependencies are minimized and referential integrity policies are accommodated.

The component interaction stage is where the full details of the system structure emerges, with a clear understanding of the dependencies between components, down to the individual operation level.

2.4.3   Component Specification

The final stage of specification is where the detailed specification of operations and constraints takes place. For a given interface it means defining the potential states of component objects in an **Interface Information Model**, and then specifying pre- and postconditions for operations, and capturing business rules as constraints. The pre- and postconditions and other constraints make reference to the types in the interface information model and the types of the parameters. In addition to these interface specification details, this stage also witnesses the specification of constraints that are specific to a particular component specification and independent of each interface. These component specification constraints determine how the type definitions in individual interfaces will correspond to each other in the context of that component.

The architecture should not materially change at this stage. This detailed specification task should be undertaken once the architecture is stable and all the operations of the interfaces have been identified. The act of writing the precise rules for each operation may help you discover missing parameters, or missing information, but the emphasis is on filling in detail onto a stable framework.

2.5 Summary

Projects follow two processes. The management process schedules work, plans deliveries, allocates resources, assesses risk, and monitors progress. The development process creates working software from requirements.

The development process, which is the subject of this book, can be divided into a number of workflows that have dependencies but that can proceed iteratively.

The requirements workflow generates a business concept model and a use case model.

The specification workflow is divided into three stages:

1. The component identification stage produces an initial component architecture from the requirements.

2. The component interaction stage discovers the operations needed and allocates responsibilities.

3. The component specification stage creates precise specifications of operations, interfaces, and components.

The provisioning workflow is responsible for delivering software conforming to the component specification it is given. This may be through implementing it, buying it, and adapting it, or by integrating and adapting existing software.

The assembly workflow links components, user interface and application logic, and existing software together into a working application.

Chapter 3

Applying UML

I n earlier chapters we explained the concepts and principles of component software and took a look at the design process we follow in this book. We also began identifying the key model artifacts that we use in the component modeling workflows. In this chapter we look at how best to use UML to represent these component concepts and model artifacts. Subsequent chapters deal with when and how to use the various UML techniques.

This book isn't a UML primer. If you don't know the basics of UML you should first read an introductory text, such as Fowler's *UML Distilled* [Fowler99].

3.1 Why Do We Need This Chapter at All?

It may seem odd to you that we need this chapter. After all, the UML has been standardized and includes the notion of "component." Why isn't that enough?

We need to make sure that we all have a common understanding of the way we use UML in this book. There are several reasons for this:

- UML was originally designed as a language for object-oriented analysis and design. Further, it is based on the assumption of an object-oriented implementation. As we explained in Chapter 1, our focus in this book is on the external aspects of software components and not their internals, irrespective of whether they are coded using an object-oriented language. In particular, we want to separate the specification aspects of design from the pure implementation choices. This special focus means that some UML features become less important, while others are stressed.

- Constructing systems with components places extra emphasis on the ability to plug software pieces together. In turn, this emphasizes the need for clear and precise interface definitions. Although our views on interface specification certainly fit within UML, they cause us to use it in new ways, which we need to explain.

- We are interested in techniques rather than diagrams: The same UML diagram can be used for a variety of purposes, and we need to explain how we use UML to support the techniques described later in the book.

- UML is designed to be extended. An important principle throughout the development of UML has been that it provides a base language that everyone can agree on, while accepting that its application to different contexts may need these base concepts either to be interpreted in different ways or to be extended to add the desired semantics.

Perhaps in the future UML will be extended to support component modeling concepts, but this book is for practitioners who need to design component systems now, using UML as it stands today (UML 1.3) and today's UML tools. Therefore we have done our utmost to stay within the current UML standard, and not include extensions and alternatives that, while arguably beneficial, are not supported by today's UML tools.

3.1.1 Tools

In some cases current versions of popular tools do support a particular concept in exactly the way we need, either because they are already thinking ahead, or because they have not implemented all the UML constraints to the letter, and therefore allow it to be flexed a little. This book does not take a position on, or recommend, any software tools. However, we have applied our techniques using a variety of current tools to ensure that what we say is practical today, and is easily achieved with those tools.

3.2 Extending UML with Stereotypes

UML has a number of extension mechanisms, but probably the most useful, at least in theory, is **Stereotypes**. Pretty much any UML element can have one stereotype attached to it; the stereotype's name then normally appears on the element enclosed by « ». Stereotypes are a way of letting users create new kinds of UML modeling elements, albeit ones that closely resemble some built-in type. For example, you might decide that you wish to distinguish between utility classes and regular classes. A simple way of doing that would be to define a «utility» stereotype for class and mark utility classes with that stereotype.

But there's more to it than that. Whenever you define a stereotype, UML allows you also to define a set of constraints that must hold for all elements marked with that stereotype. These constraints operate at the model level, so you could say that «utility» classes can have only static features, for example. At least, that's the theory. In practice, current UML tools almost never allow you to add such constraints, even in natural language, let alone something that can be checked automatically, such as object constraint language (OCL) [Warmer99]. So while it is easy to add UML extensions using stereotypes (and we'll be doing that), getting tool support for the constraints we'd like associated with those extensions is much harder.

3.3 Precision, Accuracy, and Completeness

OCL is a textual language for creating logical expressions. Despite being a full part of UML 1.3 and being used extensively in the definition of the UML itself, OCL is almost completely unsupported by current mainstream modeling tools, which is a shame because OCL allows us to be much more precise, especially when specifying component behavior.

Anyway, we use some OCL in this book, although you could manage without it, either by being less precise or by using natural language alone (which amounts to the same thing).

Using OCL improves precision but implies nothing about the complete-ness of a model. Many people confuse precision and completeness, but they aren't related. You can be very precise in the things you choose to say but leave many other things unsaid. That's the way it is (or should be) with UML models. For example, if you asked someone for a specification of their age they might say "over 30 years." This is precise, but not complete. Importantly, it's a condition that can be tested. That's what precision gives you. Contrast this with saying "I'm old." This is imprecise, because you don't know what "old" means, or your definition may not be the same as someone else's. When we're building large systems, partial models are fine, even essential.

Unfortunately, precision also doesn't imply accuracy. You can specify a software component in excruciating detail but still end up with something that totally fails to meet the need. It's always worth bearing that in mind when you are up to your elbows in OCL.

However, precision in models is useful because it allows you to test for accuracy. Once you know exactly what a model says (and what it doesn't), you're almost obliged to ask yourself whether it is right. Precise models are very good at generating test conditions.

3.4   UML Modeling Techniques

Most of the rest of this chapter is devoted to explaining how we use UML to model the various artifacts needed in component modeling. The tech-niques involved are explained in the workflow chapters. We have defined a number of diagrams corresponding to these artifacts that support these techniques, and these are shown in Figure 3.1 against the simple package structure we introduced in Chapter 2. These aren't new diagram types in the sense that they introduce any new notation—we work within the standard UML notation—but they are specific and focused usages of standard UML diagrams for particular purposes.

Perhaps the first thing to say is that when we use the term *model* for an artifact, as in "business type model," we are using it in a general-purpose way simply to mean a self-contained set of model elements. We do not mean it carries the specific semantics of a UML model, which is a com-plete abstraction of a system.

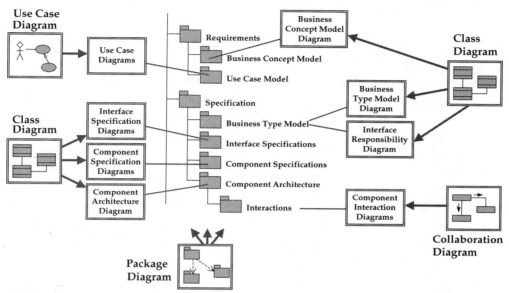

Figure 3.1   Component modeling diagrams

For the most part, the diagrams we draw bear the same names as the artifacts they visualize. For example, the **Business Concept Model Diagram** is a class diagram depicting the business concept model. An **Interface Specification Diagram** depicts an interface specification. And so it continues, with the **Business Type Model Diagram**, the **Component Specification Diagrams,** and the **Component Architecture Diagram** each depicting their corresponding artifact(s).

The only variations from the natural naming correspondence are the **Interface Responsibility Diagram** and the **Component Interaction Diagram**. The interface responsibility diagram is a class diagram depicting the business type model augmented with business interfaces and applying some rules for allocating information responsibility to those interfaces. The component interaction diagram is a collaboration diagram applied to the interaction between component objects. Each of these is explained in more detail as we go through the workflows.

As you can see from Figure 3.1, we make extensive use of the class diagram. We also use the collaboration diagram for interaction modeling, the use case diagram for use case modeling, and the package diagram to organize things.

We could use the sequence diagram as an alternative to the collaboration diagram to depict interactions, but we like the structural emphasis the collaboration diagram gives by showing the relationships between objects, and, generally, we are not modeling complicated message sequences. Remember, this is specification, not implementation. But anywhere we've used the collaboration diagram you could use the sequence diagram instead if you prefer to, or if your tool provides better support for that interaction form.

You'll notice we don't use the component diagram or deployment diagram. Again, this is because we're focusing on specification, not implementation. UML components are implementation packaging and deployment constructs, whereas we're in the business of creating component specifications, which are specification constructs. We elaborate on this a lot more as we get into the details.

We also don't use the activity diagram or the state diagram. It's not that they're not useful, it's just that we don't need them in our workflows. In certain places we discuss where such diagrams could be used to provide additional support to the techniques we're describing, or where they might be used in related workflows to the ones we're describing. In our experience, UML activity diagrams have two main uses: to describe business processes and to describe the algorithms of operations. Neither of these uses strictly fall within the scope of this book (although you'll see an activity diagram in Chapter 4 as a lead in to use case modeling and business concept modeling).

State diagrams have a worthy history in computing. They are very useful for describing sequencing constraints, and we could have used them as part of our interface specifications. However, it is possible—but not as elegant in complex cases—to use attributes and pre- and postconditions to achieve the same effect, and that's what we've done.

As a general theme, we use the class diagram in a variety of ways to capture the structural or static aspects of our specification models, and the interaction diagrams to capture the behavioral or dynamic aspects of the specification models. At the requirements level we similarly use the class diagram to capture the business concepts in the domain being studied, and the use case diagram (which can be thought of as a specialized form of interaction diagram) to understand the interaction between the users and the system.

We now go through the content of each of the models (business concept, use case, business type, interface specification, component specification, component architecture) and show how we apply UML in that context. Again, our purpose is not to explain UML but to show how we apply UML concepts to these particular artifacts. Throughout this chapter we illustrate the approach with small examples. We have kept them small and simple so that the use of UML is clear. We then develop a comprehensive case study through the more detailed workflow chapters.

3.5   Business Concept Model

The business concept model is a conceptual model. It is not a model of software, but a model of the information that exists in the problem domain. The main purpose of the business concept model diagram is to capture concepts and identify relationships. We use a UML class diagram to represent it, but it's important to note that it is a software-independent model. If you wish you could use a «concept» stereotype for every class in this model, but since, from a packaging point of view, it's kept under Requirements, and is quite separate from the Specification part of the model, we find in practice that we don't need to use a stereotype.

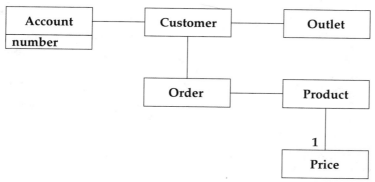

Figure 3.2   A simple business concept model

Business concept models typically capture conceptual classes and their associations. Association roles may or may not have their multiplicities specified. The model may contain attributes, if they are significant, but they need not be typed, and operations would not be used. Since the emphasis of the model is to capture domain knowledge, not to synthesize it or normalize it, you would rarely use generalization in this model. Similarly, dependency relationships would typically not be used.

3.6 Use Case Model

Love them or hate them, Use Case Models are what the UML provides for semiformal modeling of user-system interaction. Use cases are not tightly specified in UML, so you can create pretty much anything you like and describe it as a use case. Crucially, the UML does not specify the way in which use case content is described; we make that up for ourselves.

We employ use cases purely as a technique for describing the desired user-system interactions that occur at the system boundary. We recognize that use cases can validly fulfill other needs, such as modeling business operations, that are beyond the scope of this book. Use cases, the way we use them, are a projection of the requirements of a system, expressed in terms of the interactions that must occur across the system boundary.

The participants in a use case are the **Actors** and the system. An actor is an entity that interacts with the system, typically a person playing a role. It's possible for an actor to be another system, but, if it is, the details of that system are hidden from us—we see it simply as a dull and predictable person. One actor is always identified as the actor who initiates the use case; the other actors, if any, are used by the system (and sometimes the initiating actor) to meet the initiator's goal.

In a use case the actors interact with the system as a whole, not some specific part of it. The system is viewed as a homogenous black box that accepts stimuli from actors and generates responses.

It is important to distinguish between the actor and the mechanism the actor uses to communicate with the system, such as a GUI application running on a PC, a panel of buttons in an elevator, or—in the case where another system is the user—a TCP/IP connection. A use case shouldn't be concerned with the communication mechanism, only with the business meaning of the stimuli and responses.

A perennial problem with use cases is deciding their scope and size. There seems to be no consensus on this issue, but here's our view: To a first approximation we can say that a use case is smaller than a business process but larger than a single operation on a single component. The purpose of a use case is to meet the immediate goal of an actor, such as placing an order or checking a bank account balance. It includes everything that can be done now or nearly now by the system to meet the goal. For example, if it is necessary to perform an electronic credit check with an agency before accepting an order, we would expect the use case to perform the check and proceed. On the other hand, if goods need to be ordered from a supplier to fulfill the order being placed, the use case would end when the goods are ordered; it wouldn't wait for them to arrive. The subsequent arrival of the goods would stimulate another use case. We examine this issue again in Chapter 4.

To be more accurate, in UML terms our granularity characterization really only applies to base use cases. Use cases can also be extended by other use cases and include other use cases, and these others will necessarily be of finer granularity than their base. In UML, the base element, the extensions, and the inclusions are model elements of type use case.

3.6.1   Use Case Diagrams

Use Case Diagrams, with their familiar stick figures and ellipses, are useful only as a catalogue or map. Use cases can be defined with a number of extension points to which extension use cases refer. This approach is useful for defining the broad structure of the use case in a diagram (see Figure 3.3) but still leaves the real detail of the use case to be captured in textual use case descriptions (see Figure 3.4).

3.6.2   Use Case Descriptions

The textual structure we prefer is based on that of Alistair Cockburn (see [CockburnWeb]). We present a simplified form here. A **Use Case Description** contains at least

- an identifying name and/or number
- the name of the initiating actor

- a short description of the goal of the use case
- a single numbered sequence of steps that describe the main success scenario

Except in the case of an inclusion step, each step takes the form "A does X," where A is an actor or the system. The first step must indicate the

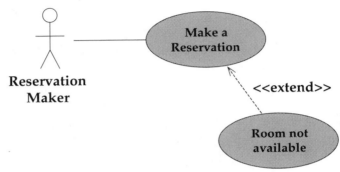

Figure 3.3 Simple use case diagram

Name	Make a Reservation
Initiator	Reservation Maker
Goal	Reserve a room at a hotel

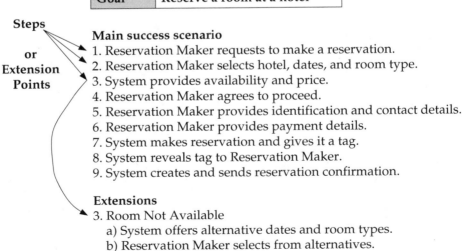

Steps
or
Extension
Points

Main success scenario
1. Reservation Maker requests to make a reservation.
2. Reservation Maker selects hotel, dates, and room type.
3. System provides availability and price.
4. Reservation Maker agrees to proceed.
5. Reservation Maker provides identification and contact details.
6. Reservation Maker provides payment details.
7. System makes reservation and gives it a tag.
8. System reveals tag to Reservation Maker.
9. System creates and sends reservation confirmation.

Extensions
3. Room Not Available
   a) System offers alternative dates and room types.
   b) Reservation Maker selects from alternatives.

Figure 3.4 Textual description of a use case

stimulus that initiates the use case (i.e., what the initiating actor does to indicate to the system that it wants this goal met). The combination of initiating actor and stimulus must be unique across all use cases.

The main success scenario describes what happens in the most common case and when nothing goes wrong. It is broken into a number of separate **Use Case Steps**. The assumption is that the steps are performed strictly sequentially in the order given—unlike most business process languages there is no way of describing parallelism, which is one reason why a use case is typically smaller than a business process. Each use case step acts as a UML use case extension point. It is the anchor point from which an extend relationship to an extension use case may be defined.

Use case steps are always written in natural language. Use cases are a semiformal technique and must be understandable by anyone familiar with the problem domain.

3.6.3   Use Case Instances

A use case description is a template for behavior that is instantiated in the environment of a deployed system each time an actor generates a stimulus. A **Use Case Instance** either succeeds or fails in meeting the goal. A simple use case consisting only of a main success scenario is assumed always to succeed.

3.6.4   Inclusions, Extensions, and Variations

One use case can **Include** another by naming it in a step. This means that when an instance of the including use case reaches that step, it invokes the included use case and then proceeds to the next step.

Extensions are a mechanism for semiformal specification of alternatives or additions to the main success scenario.[1] Each extension is described separately, after the main success scenario. An extension comprises the following:

- The step number (i.e., extension point) in the main success scenario at which the extension applies.

---

1. Strictly speaking, each extension describes a new use case that participates in an **Extend** relationship with the main use case.

- A condition that must be tested before that step. If the condition is true the extension is activated; if false the extension is ignored and the main success scenario continues as usual.

- A numbered sequence of steps that constitute the extension.

The steps in an extension can take any of the two forms found in the main success scenario: "A does X" or "useCaseReference" (to include the use case with that name or number). In addition, the last step in an extension can take one of the following forms:

- **Fail**—to indicate the use case is terminated with the goal unsatisfied

- **Stop**—to indicate that the use case is terminated with the goal satisfied

- **Resume N**—to indicate the next step to be performed in the main success scenario

If the last step of the extension is not one of these, the main success scenario continues with its normal next step (i.e., no step is skipped—the extension does not replace a step in the main success scenario).

Sometimes we know that there will be some significant variations in the flow of a use case but we don't want to specify them all now as extensions. So we can include at the end of the use case description a list of **Variations**. A variation is just a free text note saying that the variation can occur.

Please see [Cockburn00] for a much more detailed template for use cases.

3.7   Business Type Model

The **Business Type Model** is a specification model. It is modeled using a UML class diagram but its purpose is quite different to that of the concept model. The business type model is concerned with modeling precisely the business information that is relevant to the scope of the envisaged system. Naturally, many of its classes bear the same names as classes in the concept model, but they do not represent the same thing. For example, the business concept model may contain a class called "customer," which represents the concept of customer in the business domain. By contrast, the class "customer" in the business type model represents the system's understanding of customer, which is typically scoped down and more precisely defined.

3.7.1 Types

To indicate that the classes in the business type model are specification-level, we use the built-in stereotype «type» for them. This makes it very clear that it is not a model of programming language classes. Note, though, that in our business type models the types can't have operations because they describe only information, not software, whereas the built-in stereotype «type» does allow operations.

The business type model is intended to represent precisely the information about the business with which the system will need to be concerned. This means it's useful to remove redundancy and make use of generalization where it aids understanding. But it is not a database design. Don't start thinking about normal forms or worrying about one-to-one associations. Remember it's a specification model—it's a set of rules.

Attributes

Attributes must be typed, and the type must be a data type. Visibility is irrelevant in a specification model, since nothing is internal or private, so it's best set to "public." As a matter of style we prefer all our attribute names to begin with a lowercase letter.

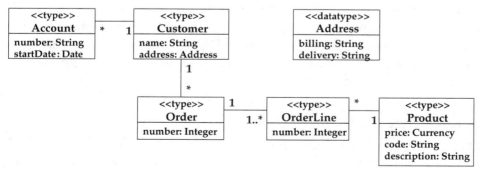

Figure 3.5 A simple business type model

Associations

As with attributes, association roles should have public visibility, and the role names, if explicitly stated, should begin with a lowercase letter. In the business type model we reserve the use of navigability (arrows on associations) to indicate responsibility for holding inter-interface associations, as explained in Chapter 5.

We don't find we need to use qualified associations, and there aren't any in the case study.

Although using composition is fine, we recommend against using aggregation unless you're certain you know what it means (which can only mean you've defined it for yourself. See Henderson-Sellers' UML 99 conference paper [Sellers99] for a gruesome dissection of the semantics of UML aggregation).

Meaning of Attribute and Association

It's important to remember that type models are specification models. They don't represent object-oriented programming classes or relational database tables (although mappings to such implementation constructs are very valuable). In a business type model, an attribute or association role describes a piece of data related to the type named in the rectangle. It represents information that the business needs to maintain and corresponds to a question you might validly ask, "What is the order number of this order?"

Collectively, the attributes and association roles define a set of **Queries** that can be applied to a type when writing specification constraints in OCL. They are a formalized vocabulary for referring to information. They do *not* represent a shorthand for get and set operations of an interface or an implementation class. The specification of operations of components is the job of the interface, not the business type.

Parameterized Attributes

Once you're comfortable with the idea of specification attributes as a tool to help define constraints, you're ready to consider parameterized attributes. A **Parameterized Attribute** is one whose value depends on the values of its parameters. For example, a person's contact number might be dependent on the day of the week. So rather than have an attribute

```
contactNumber: String
```

we can define

```
contactNumber(day: Day): String
```

It's not an operation—it's not specifying something that a client could call or invoke or send a message to—it's simply a specification query to support the definition of constraints.

The bad news is that UML doesn't support this concept. However, it is so useful that this is an area where we're prepared to twist the UML a little. Since our regular «type» doesn't have operations (these belong to interfaces) this leaves type "operations" available for use as parameterized attributes. They must be defined as functions, always having a return value. Depending on your tool interchange requirements, it may be useful to mark these operations as attributes using a stereotype like «att». In practice, we usually leave it off. An example of how this would look as a UML class is shown in Figure 3.6.

Note: This concept should not be confused with the UML concept of a query operation, which is a true operation but one that is read-only and has no side effects.

For further details, Catalysis [D'Souza99] gives a thorough treatment of this subject.

3.7.2   Structured Data Types

The notion of a data type is defined in UML, but we want to call out the use of structured data types explicitly. We use UML classes again to define

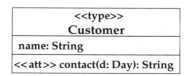

Figure 3.6   Parameterized attribute

structured data types, such as Address in Figure 3.5, and we use the «datatype» stereotype for these. This stereotype defines certain constraints: The data type may not have associations, or operations, and its attributes must also be typed as data types (simple or structured). During interface specification we also allow attributes to be references to component objects (i.e., to be of type interface).

3.7.3   Interface Type

As we develop the business type model we add interface types to it. We use a stereotyped class to represent an interface at the specification level; the stereotype is called «interface type». We have also adopted the convention of prefacing the names of interfaces with "I."

Meaning of Attribute and Association

As for all types, the attributes and association roles of an interface are for the purpose of specification only. They do *not* imply the existence of operations that can retrieve the results of the queries; if such operations are required they must be defined explicitly. When we reach the detailed specification stage for interfaces, we define its set of attributes and association roles, and their types, as its **Interface Information Model**. The purpose of this model is to support the full specification of an interface, and we discuss that later in this chapter.

The UML «interface»

You may be aware that the UML standard includes a predefined modeling element called Interface that you can use in class diagrams: Because it is a kind of Classifier it is drawn like a class with an «interface» stereotype. Why aren't we using it?

Well, UML interfaces are really designed for modeling object-oriented implementation language constructs, notably the interface concept found in Java. They also accommodate the runtime component environment concept of interface as found in Microsoft COM and CORBA. Since UML interfaces have this implementation focus they do not have attributes or associations, and we'd like our interfaces to have both, because we have a specification focus. Of course, you might be using a modeling tool that doesn't enforce these UML restrictions, in which case you are free to use «interface», but you would be bending the UML standard.

A useful way of thinking about the relationship between an interface type and a UML interface is to consider a UML interface as a potential realization of an interface type, in the usual "implementation realizes specification" sense. Figure 3.7 shows a customer management interface type mapping onto (or being realized by) a customer management interface in an implementation model. The implementation interface could be more specifically stereotyped as, say, «java interface» or «COM interface» to allow the constraints of those technologies to be applied.

We use the UML concept of interface in Chapter 8 when we show examples of mapping specification to implementation and discuss technology bindings.

In order to avoid verbosity in the text we generally use the term "interface" to mean "interface type," since we're mostly talking about the specification world. Where we discuss both the specification and implementation spaces together we are explicit.

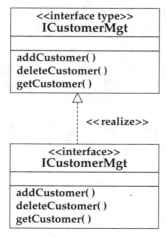

Figure 3.7 Interface types and interfaces

3.7.4   Invariants

UML defines an invariant as a stereotype of Constraint, which applies to classifiers and their relationships. For our purposes, an invariant is therefore a constraint on a type model, and we often use such constraints within business type models. We usually write invariants using the OCL.

An invariant is like a rule about the instances, so at the specification level many of the invariants you specify correspond to business rules. For this reason it's worth managing them carefully and maintaining them.

Figure 3.8 shows an IOrder interface, with an orderNo attribute and some operations.

We want to specify that order numbers are always greater than zero. We can do that with an invariant as shown: orderNo > 0.

An invariant is a constraint that applies to all instances of a type. This is interpreted as "for all component objects supporting the IOrder interface, at all times when the system is quiescent (i.e., not in the process of changing state) it is the case that the value of their orderNo attribute is greater than zero." The invariant shown is actually a shorthand for

```
self.orderNo > 0
```

where self is an anonymous object supporting the interface. The invariant is saying that the condition must hold when self is any object supporting the interface. OCL allows us to omit the self when the meaning is clear.

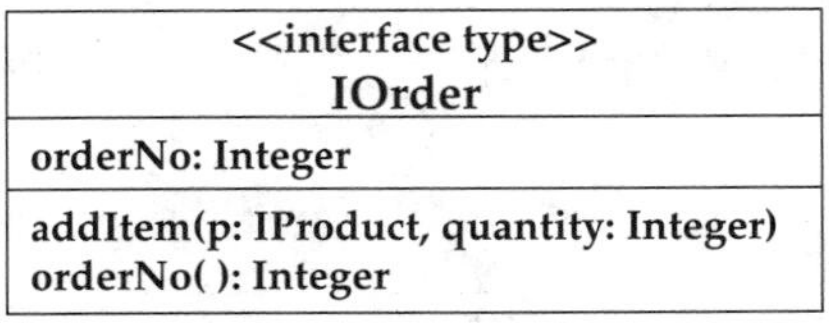

<<interface type>> **IOrder**
orderNo: Integer
addItem(p: IProduct, quantity: Integer) **orderNo( ): Integer**

```
context IOrder
invariant:
-- order number is a positive integer
orderNo > 0

-- orderNo() returns orderNo
orderNo() = orderNo
```

Figure 3.8   Invariants on IOrder

In addition, we want to specify that the result of the operation orderNo( ) is always the value of the orderNo attribute. The invariant for this is

```
orderNo() = orderNo
```

Note that we distinguish operations from attributes by always following an operation with parentheses, even if it has no parameters.

It won't have escaped your notice that much of this detailed OCL specification is done using text. In our examples we've used note boxes linked to the appropriate element in the diagram. If your tool provides specific places to hold invariant and operation specifications you can put them there. It might be useful, though, to check that your tool provides a sensible way of reporting or displaying this information together with the type model to which they apply—the value of seeing the constraints adjacent to the diagram is not to be underestimated.

3.8 Interface Specification

An **Interface Specification** is an interface together with all the other specification paraphernalia needed to define precisely what a component that offers that interface must do, and what a client of that interface can expect. An interface specification consists of these parts:

- The interface type itself
- Its information model—the attributes and association roles of the interface, and their types, transitively until closure
- Its operation specifications—operation signatures and pre- and postconditions
- Any additional invariants on the information model

3.8.1 Interface Specification Package

We group all this specification information into a single package—so each interface specification has its own package. This package may import specification information from other packages. For example, in

Figure 3.9 we have defined a specification package for the customer management interface ICustomerMgt. It contains the interface itself, the types it's associated with (in this case Customer), and any data types needed. Some data types, such as CustDetails, will be exclusive to the interface specification and so would normally be placed in the same package. Others, like Address, might be more generic and imported from shared packages of types. Still others, like common built-in types such as String, might be globally or implicitly available and would not need explicit import.

If you are using interface inheritance you can still retain the packaging structure and exclusive type ownership by importing the supertype's package into the subtype's package.

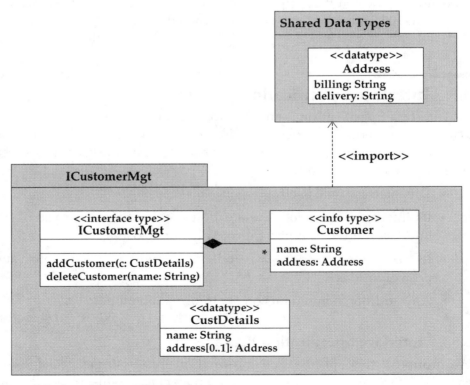

Figure 3.9   Interface specification package

3.8.2 Information Model

One of the goals of component modeling is to define relatively independent interface specifications. So whereas in the business type model we had a single integrated type model, when specifying interfaces we seek to define a number of independent type models, one for each interface. The types in these models are exclusive to their interface (that is to say, the nondata type ones are), and represent a projection or refinement of the type information in the business type model. Each interface has its own view of the information it cares about. For this reason we call these types **Information Types**, to distinguish them from the business types in the business type model, and we give them the «info type» stereotype.

We depict the information model of an interface in an interface specification diagram. This shows all the types in the information model and is a key diagram during the detailed operation specification tasks. When writing the pre- and postconditions of the interface's operations, it is essential you have this diagram in front of you.

So the business type model consists of business types (and interfaces), whereas an interface information model consists of an interface and an exclusive set of information types. Information types are the most common kind of type, so in our case study diagrams we've chosen not to display the stereotype name, to avoid clutter.

3.8.3 Operation Specification

An operation specification consists of a signature and a pre- and postcondition pair.

Signature

An operation defined on an interface has a signature comprising zero or more typed parameters. The type of a parameter can be

- a reference to a component object; the type of the parameter will typically be an interface
- a simple data type, such as an integer
- a structured data type, such as CustDetails
- a collection of any of these

Data types are always passed by value; values have no identity and cannot be shared between the operation invoker and implementer—each must have its own copy.

Pre- and Postcondition Pair

In UML, operation pre- and postconditions are defined as constraints on that operation, with the stereotypes «precondition» and «postcondition», respectively. Since they're constraints we normally write them in OCL.

A precondition is a Boolean expression that is evaluated—theoretically—before the operation executes; a postcondition is a Boolean expression that is evaluated after the operation finishes. We say *theoretically* because the pre- and postconditions are specification artifacts—they aren't embodied in the final code. The idea is that if the precondition is true, the postcondition must also be true. If the precondition is false, the behavior is undefined. We cover pre- and postconditions in more detail in Chapter 7.

Transactional Behavior

An important topic when specifying operations for distributed component systems is their transactional behavior, but this is not covered in UML. The various component environments (COM, EJB, CORBA Component Model) provide relatively rich schemes for the definition of transactional behavior. We need to specify transactional requirements in a way that readily maps onto these technologies.

In business information systems pretty much everything is transactional. The specification issue therefore boils down to whether an operation starts its own transaction or runs in an existing transaction. Since this is a binary choice we can model it simply by defining an operation stereotype for one of the cases. We choose to call out the forced new transaction case and we define a stereotype «transaction» for it. Absence of the stereotype then implies that an operation runs in an existing transaction.

3.9 Component Specification

In Chapter 1 we discussed the meaning of "component" in some detail and described a variety of different component forms. The UML concept of component is geared toward the implementation and deployment world. Within that domain it is very flexible (some would say too flexible) and can be used to accommodate a number of our more tightly defined forms, specifically Component Implementation and Installed Component. But our focus in this book is on specification. We need to represent the Component Specification form, and the UML component construct doesn't fit the bill.

We therefore define a component specification as another stereotype of class, called «comp spec». Like the distinction in Figure 3.7 between a UML interface and an «interface type» class, a UML component realizes a «comp spec» class (see Figure 3.10).

A component specification offers a set of interface types. At the implementation level this "offers" relationship is modeled as a realization of a set of interfaces by a component. But "realization" is not the correct semantics here. We therefore define a new stereotype of UML dependency called «offers» to capture this important relationship (see Figure 3.11).

Notationally, we would like our interface types to have the option of being displayed as "lollipops," just as UML defines for interfaces. UML

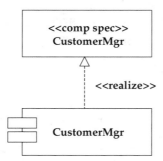

Figure 3.10 UML components realize component specifications

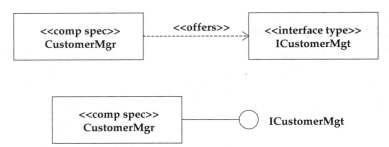

Figure 3.11 Component specifications offer interface types, with "lollipop" notation

allows you to define an icon for any stereotyped element so this fits quite nicely.[2]

A component specification is the building block of a component architecture. It addition to the set of interfaces it offers, it defines the set of interfaces it must use. This is an architectural constraint, not a component design choice. We model this with a simple UML usage dependency. A usage dependency between a component specification and an interface type specifies that all realizations of the component must use that interface. For example, in Figure 3.12 we specify that the customer manager component must use an address management interface. It doesn't specify which component it must use, just which interfaces. Binding these interfaces to the actual components is an architecture task.

We call Figure 3.12 a component specification diagram. It focuses on a single component specification and details its individual dependencies.

A component specification also defines any constraints that it requires between these interfaces, and any constraints on the implementation of its operations. These operation implementation constraints can be defined using component interactions.

---

2. From a tool point of view, as we discussed earlier, you may choose to use the UML interface concept as if it were an interface type, but only if the tool doesn't impose all the constraints that UML demands. You'll then be in a position where you might be (ab)using the realize relationship between a «comp spec» class and an interface to represent the "component spec offers interface type" relationship. Ideally your tool would allow you to define that a «comp spec» class cannot be the target of a realize dependency. But if it doesn't, and you've explicitly decided to use the relationship in this way, you'll need to take care.

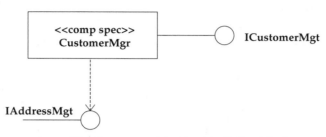

Figure 3.12 Component specification, an architecture building block

3.9.1   Component Object Interaction

We use UML collaboration diagrams to specify the desired interactions between component objects. These component interaction diagrams can focus on one particular component object and show how it uses the interfaces of other component objects. Or they can be used to depict an extended set of interacting component objects in a complete architecture.

The rectangles in the diagrams represent component objects that support the interfaces shown. Since components can support many interfaces it is quite possible that two or more rectangles represent the same object. The links must be instances of associations between interfaces that are part of the interface specification or component specification, unless they are transient (i.e., they exist no longer than the duration of the collaboration).

Figure 3.13 shows an interaction diagram for the getAddress() operation on a CustomerMgr component object supporting ICustomerMgt, passing in a customer Id and getting back some address details. In turn, it calls getAddress() on a component object supporting IAddressMgt (note the signature has changed—it's not the same operation). It passes an internal address Id it is holding and gets back the address details, which it can then process as needed and pass back.

Let's have a look at the object naming here. In UML, the naming rules for roles in a collaboration are objectname/rolename:classifiername. We're using anonymous instances so our object names are blank. Then we adjust things to add component semantics—the idea is to consider an interface as the role of a component object in an interaction. So, for the role names of the objects we use the interface names directly, and for the classifier name we identify the component specification offering that interface. If it is blank, we are leaving it unspecified.

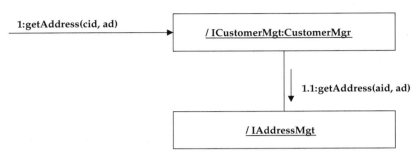

Figure 3.13   A component interaction diagram

So /ICustomerMgt:CustomerMgr specifies an instance of the CustomerMgr component playing an ICustomerMgt role. /IAddressMgt identifies an unspecified component object playing that role.

In an interaction diagram, only component objects for which we identify the component specification can send messages, because message sending is a function of the component, not an interface. The object /IAddressMgt in Figure 3.13 has no component specification indicated, so we couldn't show any outgoing messages from it.

When we use an interaction diagram to specify an individual component, we only show direct interactions between objects of the type being specified and objects supporting the interfaces it uses—we never show subsequent downstream interactions.

Even in software things don't happen without cause, so every interaction diagram should show, as an incoming arrow to one of the rectangles, the stimulus that causes the interaction. Figure 3.13 shows an interaction that begins when an object supporting the ICustomerMgt interface receives a getAddress( ) message. This is the first message and so is labeled 1. Subsequent messages then follow a nested-numbering scheme.

3.9.2   Specification, Not Implementation

You may be wondering why we use collaboration diagrams at all. After all, didn't we say that we are interested only in specifying the externals of the components, not the details of their internal implementations? It looks as though collaboration diagrams are all about internal design decisions. In

Figure 3.13, surely what the CustomerMgr component does in its implementation of the getAddress( ) operation is an internal design decision?

Well, if the implementer really does have a free choice about how best to implement the operation, we shouldn't draw this collaboration (at least not as a specification level diagram). As specifiers, we draw collaborations specifically to restrict the freedom of the implementation designer. Figure 3.13 is part of the contract between the specifier and the realizer that we discussed in Chapter 1. It says "whatever else the realization of getAddress( ) does, it must invoke the getAddress( ) operation of the associated IAddressMgt object." We are reducing the options for the realizer, to create a stable architecture into which a variety of alternative realizations can be plugged. All the realizations must conform to these restrictions.

As we show in Chapter 7, it is sometimes possible to express these constraints declaratively, rather than through the procedural mechanism of a collaboration diagram.

3.10 Component Architectures

As described in Chapter 1, we define a number of different component architectures, namely component specification architectures, component implementation architectures, and component object architectures. From the point of view of applying UML, these introduce no new ideas: They are simply diagrams that depict many components rather than just one.

A component architecture defines a context within which the interface usage dependencies of standalone component specifications are bound to the «offers» dependencies of other standalone component specifications. So, instead of a number of independent component specifications we have a single component architecture. We call the type of diagram shown in Figure 3.14 a component architecture diagram. This one shows a component specification architecture (we can tell that from the «comp spec» stereotypes). The same form (using the standard UML notation of underlining for instances) can be used to show a component object architecture.

We can also draw these diagrams without the interfaces to give a coarser-grain view (see Figure 3.15). It's unnecessary for this simple example, but for

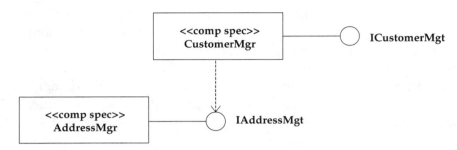

Figure 3.14   A component specification architecture

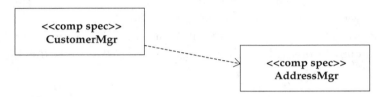

Figure 3.15   Component architecture showing dependencies at the component specification level

large architectures with many components, interfaces, and dependencies, it's a valuable abstraction.

We also draw component interaction diagrams within an architectural context, to understand how the components will work together and to discover the operations that are needed. If you know the broad shape of your architecture and your likely interfaces, the best way of figuring out the operations those interfaces need is to work through the collaborations. This process is discussed in detail in Chapter 6.

3.11   Summary

Congratulations. You've learned pretty much every bit of UML you'll need to do component specification with UML and to understand the case study. We've introduced the stereotypes we need and any constraints they have. We've described the types of diagram we need to draw. And we've

Table 3.1 Summary of UML extensions

Component Specification Concept	UML Construct	Stereotype
Component Specification	Class	«comp spec»
Interface Type	Type (Class «type»)	«interface type»
Comp Spec offers Interface Type	Dependency	«offers»
Business Concept	Class	«concept» (optional)
Business Type	Type (Class «type»)	«type»
Structured Data Type	Type (Class «type»)	«datatype»
Interface Information Type	Type (Class «type»)	«info type» (often omitted)
Parameterized Attribute	Operation	«att»
Operation requiring a new transaction	Operation	«transaction»

only had to extend UML a couple of places to fit. It's fair to say that UML has stood up pretty well to our requirements of it.

Table 3.1 summarizes the UML extensions we'll be using.

The most practical issue, of course, will be how strictly your tools support UML and what tool-interchange requirements you have. Standardizing on this set of UML extensions as a component specification profile would be a valuable step forward.

Chapter 4

Requirements Definition

T his isn't a book about requirements gathering, and we're rather relieved about that. It's not that requirements gathering is unimportant; in fact, you could validly argue that there is nothing *more* important. But effective requirements gathering is hard and full of uncertainties. It is very easy to become obsessed with "getting the requirements right" even though experience tells us they will change before we're done. Also, few sponsors of software development can remain calm through weeks (or months!) of detailed requirements capture. They want something built. Now. And, broadly, we agree with them.

So we are going to limit ourselves here to discussing how to create the minimum deliverables needed as input into the specification workflow. We aren't going to tell you how to interview users or run requirements workshops. And we certainly aren't going to tell you how much of any of that you should do. But we are going to insist you get clear on the purpose and goal of the software before you start building it.

Many organizations are trying to allow Web access to existing systems or are integrating existing systems to deliver enhanced capabilities to their clients. What is not always obvious in such developments is that the business processes needed for Web-enabled systems are usually different to the current processes. Even when 95 percent of the software capability comes from existing systems it is extremely beneficial to begin by understanding the new business processes. Of course, the temptation is to do otherwise. The temptation is to work outward from the existing systems. The inevitable result is that an understanding of the new processes emerges late in the project, and support for them gets jury-rigged into the solution, building in inflexibility right from the start.

4.1 Business Processes

We assume that you understand the business processes you want to support. For any nontrivial process it makes sense to document the process with a diagram, such as the one in Figure 4.1.

This diagram has been drawn using the UML activity diagram notation (or a close approximation to it) but that is not important—you should use whatever notation you are familiar with. How you discovered that this is the required process isn't our concern here, either, but you probably worked with users, business analysts, and domain experts to come up with it.

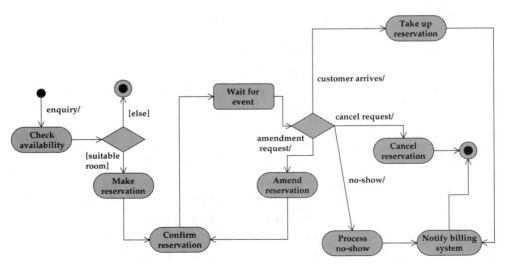

Figure 4.1 Business process for hotel reservation

The diagram in Figure 4.1 describes the process of reserving a hotel room. We are going to use this as the basis for a case study that we follow through each of the workflow chapters. In our case study, the reservation process is initiated by an enquiry from a potential customer, who states her needs. Room availability is checked and if a suitable room is available the customer makes a reservation. Details of the reservation are confirmed to the customer by e-mail. Then one of four things can happen: The customer might arrive and take up her reservation; she might cancel it; she might amend some details of it, which will require another confirmation; or she might just not turn up (no-show), but she's going to get a bill anyway. We use this example in this and subsequent chapters to illustrate the process of component system design.

The first thing to understand is that the business process description is in no way a statement of the requirements for an IT system. For one thing, the process gives no indication as to which of the activities are to be automated. It also tells us nothing about the required quality of service. But at least it lets us get started.

4.2 Business Concept Model

The business process description introduces a number of terms, such as *reservation, room,* and *customer,* which we need to get clear about. We can construct a mind map that relates these and other important terms. We call that map a **Business Concept Model**, and we can depict it using a form of UML class diagram, as described in Chapter 3. Please bear in mind that, despite using the class diagram notation, this model is not in any way related to software. It is true that there might be some elements in the software that have the same names, but that is a design decision; it doesn't follow automatically. A possible business concept model for this domain is shown in Figure 4.2. The business concept model is one of the two inputs we need for the specification workflow.

It isn't clear whether bills and payments are relevant for a reservation system, but that doesn't matter right now. The business concept model doesn't have to be tightly scoped to the problem; we do that later in the

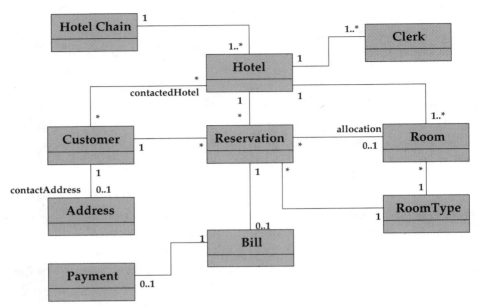

Figure 4.2 Business concept model for hotel reservation

specification workflow. Also, the business concept model doesn't need to be detailed. Here we haven't shown any attributes, but we can show them if they arise naturally during the creation of the model.

So now we know that for any hotel there will be one or more associated rooms. But do we know what a hotel and a room are? Mostly we assume that the name is sufficient to explain the purpose of the thing but really we shouldn't be so lax. For example, if a room can be partitioned into two, is that one room or two? And think about customers: How long does someone remain a customer? We're not going to go into detail here, but the right way to answer these questions formally is to use **Designations**, as explained in Jackson's book *Software Requirements & Specifications* [Jackson95], which we urge you to read. Briefly, a designation is an association between a designated term (such as *customer*) and a recognition rule (so you know a customer when you see one). However, for the purposes of this example we follow the time-honored tradition of assuming you understand what the model means because "it's obvious." (Consultants: please form a line here.)

4.3   System Envisioning

An important task in requirements capture is making clear which functions are the responsibility of the software. This is often called *defining the software boundary*. To define this boundary we need to decide from the point of view of its users, how does this system work? What will its creation mean to them? This is sometimes called **System Envisioning** and is a much under-explored area [Hodgson99].

Here's a high-level system envisioning statement for the reservation system:

> A hotel reservation system is required that will allow reservations to be made for any hotel in the chain. At present each hotel has its own, incompatible, system. Reservations can be made by telephone to a dedicated central reservation center, by telephone direct to a hotel, or via the Internet. A major advantage of the new system will be the ability to offer rooms at alternative hotels when the desired hotel is full. Within a hotel, facilities for making reservations will exist at the front desk, in the office, and at the concierge's desk. Each hotel has a reservation administrator who is responsible for controlling reservations at the hotel, but any authorized user may make a reservation. The target time for making a reservation by telephone or in person is three minutes. To speed up the process, details of previous customers will be stored and made available.

The full envisioning activity would go further, using techniques such as storyboarding, to make clear to the users of the future system exactly how they will be affected by its introduction.

4.4   Use Cases

We can now make an initial attempt at allocating responsibility for the process steps in the business process definition, as shown in Figure 4.3. We have shown the responsibilities by creating swim lanes—areas of the diagram with distinct subjects of responsibility.

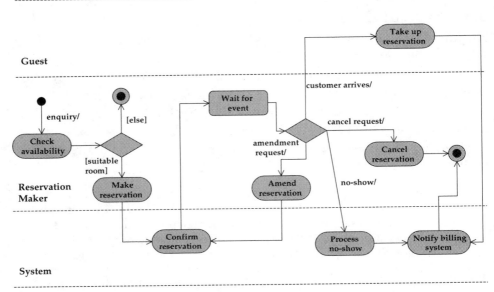

Figure 4.3   Business process with responsibilities

We decide that it is the responsibility of the software system to confirm reservations, process no-shows, and notify the billing system. By that we mean that the system will perform those functions without assistance. Other choices are possible. We could have decided that confirming a reservation was a human responsibility. Similarly, we could have decided that the details of a hotel stay are to be transferred manually to the billing system. These kinds of responsibility decisions are quick to make but have a profound effect on the shape of the resulting system. They are often taken too quickly.

4.4.1   Actors and Roles

All the other steps must be the responsibility of actors—people or external systems—outside the software. Of course, the software will probably (but not necessarily) play a part in these steps; it's just that the actor is responsible for initiating and controlling them. It's possible that these actors are already shown on the business concept model, but it's more likely that the actors are roles played by things in the business concept model.

We don't want to constrain the requirements so that only clerks can make reservations: This is the twenty-first century, after all, and customers should be able to make their own reservations if they want. So we create an actor called *ReservationMaker,* and give that actor responsibility for the main parts of making a reservation. It's tempting to make customers responsible for taking up a reservation, but we prefer to generalize the roles to cover other cases, so we define an actor called *Guest.*

We can show how the actors relate to our business concept model using generalization, as in Figure 4.4. We use UML generalization to show the "can play the role of" relationship.

4.4.2   Use Case Identification

Use cases are the primary mechanism in UML for defining the software boundary. But they go further than that: They also allow us to say how the software will meet its responsibilities. Creating use cases requires us to go further in system envisioning. You might reasonably argue that by creating use cases we are going beyond what is strictly a statement of requirements. Use cases show how the requirements are to be met by the software system. They are really a functional specification of the software system, treating the software as a black box with respect to its internal structure and organization.

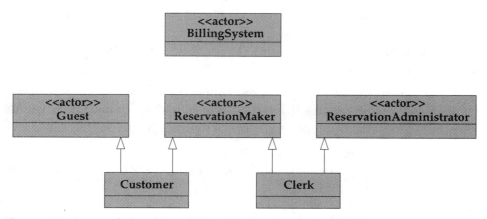

Figure 4.4   Actor relationships within a business concept model

Recall from Chapter 3 that, for us, a use case describes the interaction that follows from a single business event. Where an event triggers a number of process steps, all the steps form a single use case. The business process tells us about five events, so we can assume use cases for each of these:

1. Make Reservation (covering the Check Availability, Make Reservation, and Confirm Reservation steps)

2. Cancel Reservation

3. Amend Reservation (covering Amend Reservation and Confirm Reservation)

4. Take Up Reservation (covering Take Up Reservation and Notify Billing System)

5. Process No-Show (covering Process No-Show and Notify Billing System)

The first four seem straightforward but the last needs some thought. Not turning up is a bit of a nonevent. Exactly when does that event happen? What causes the software to process a reservation as a no-show? Probably there is a business rule, such as "A reservation not claimed by 8 a.m. on the day after scheduled arrival will be treated as a no-show." So we have a choice: We can make this processing automatic, triggered by the clock, or we can require it to be initiated by a user, as a batch activity. We choose the latter. So the use case becomes **Process No-Shows**, because it deals with all reservations that meet the no-show business rule. Who, then, is the actor who initiates this use case? We define a new actor, called ReservationAdministrator, to handle it. You probably noticed this actor already in Figure 4.4.

Armed with these five initial use cases, it is time to conduct an audit. We pore over the business concept model, asking these questions:

- Do the things these boxes represent get created and destroyed? Does the software need to know about this? If so, how does it find out? Does this thing have attributes that might change?

- Do the relationships between these things, as indicated by the associations, change over time? If so, does the software need to know and how does it find out?

We answer these questions in Tables 4.1 and 4.2.

We assume that all the things in our model might have attributes that can change, so the full list of use cases, so far as we know now, is as follows:

- Make Reservation
- Cancel Reservation
- Amend Reservation
- Take Up Reservation
- Process No-Shows
- Add/Amend/Remove Hotel

Table 4.1 Business concept model create/destroy check

HotelChain	The requirement is a reservation system for a single chain, so we never create or destroy chains.
Hotel	Hotels might be added or removed, albeit infrequently, so we will need use cases for these events.
Room	Rooms might be added or removed, so we need use cases for these events.
RoomType	Room types might be added or removed, so we need use cases for these events.
Clerk	Clerks will come and go, so we need use cases for these events. (Assuming the software needs to know about clerks—we assume it does.)
Customer	Customers become known to the software as part of the process of making a reservation. We need a housekeeping facility to remove dormant customers.
Address	Same as for customer.
Reservation	Reservations are created during the business process. We want the software to remember completed reservations for a year, so we will need a housekeeping facility to remove expired reservations.
Payment	Outside the scope of a reservation system.
Bill	Outside the scope of a reservation system.

- Add/Amend/Remove Room
- Add/Amend/Remove Room Type
- Add/Amend/Remove Clerk
- Amend Customer
- Remove Dormant Customers
- Amend Address
- Remove Old Reservations

Figure 4.5 shows a use case diagram for the reservation system. To save space we've collapsed all the add/amend/remove use cases into one.

Table 4.2 Business concept model association update check

HotelChain-Hotel	Never changes.
Hotel-Room	Never changes (can't move a room from one hotel to another).
Hotel-Clerk	Clerks can move from one hotel to another but we decide that the software won't support this. The details will need to be re-entered.
Hotel-Customer	Not to be maintained in the software.
Hotel-Reservation	Can be changed as part of reservation amendment.
Customer-Address	Never changes (but the details of an address might change).
Customer-Reservation	Never changes.
Reservation-RoomType	Can be changed as part of reservation amendment.
Reservation-Bill	Out of the scope of the system.
Reservation-Room	An interesting one! We decide (after much consultation with the domain experts) that this association is made when the customer arrives to take up his or her reservation. There will be no preallocation of rooms.
Bill-Payment	Out of the scope of the system.
RoomType-Room	Never changes (can't change a single room to a double).

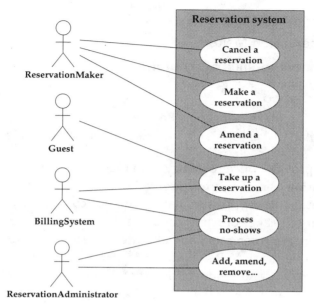

Figure 4.5   Use case diagram

4.4.3   Use Case Descriptions

Now we can create use case descriptions for two of these use cases. To do this we think about how the initiator will interact with the system. We are guided by the business process descriptions and the envisioning statement. Begin with the main success scenario, then add extensions and variations.

Name	**Make a reservation**
Initiator	**Reservation Maker**
Goal	**Reserve room(s) at a hotel**

Main Success Scenario

1. Reservation Maker asks to make a reservation.
2. Reservation Maker selects, in any order, hotel, dates, and room type.
3. System provides price to Reservation Maker.
4. Reservation Maker asks for reservation.
5. Reservation Maker provides name and post code (zip code).
6. Reservation Maker provides contact e-mail address.
7. System makes reservation and allocates tag to reservation.
8. System reveals tag to Reservation Maker.
9. System creates and sends confirmation by e-mail.

Extensions

3. Room not available.
   a. System offers alternatives.
   b. Reservation Maker selects from alternatives.
3b. Reservation Maker rejects alternatives.
   a. Fail
4. Reservation Maker declines offer.
   a. Fail
6. Customer already on file (based on name and post code).
   a. Resume 7.

Name **Take up reservation**

Initiator **Guest**

Goal **Claim a reservation and check in to the hotel**

Main Success Scenario

1. Guest arrives at hotel and claims a reservation.
2. Guest provides reservation tag.
3. Guest confirms details of stay duration, room type.
4. System allocates room.
5. System notifies billing system that a stay is starting.

Extensions

3. System cannot find a reservation with the given tag.
   a. Guest provides name and post code.
   b. System identifies guest and displays active reservations for that customer.
   c. Guest selects the reservation.
   d. Resume 4.
3. The reservation tag refers to a reservation at a different hotel.
   a2. Fail
3c. No active reservations at this hotel for this customer.
   a. Fail

Variations

At 4 the Guest may wish to change stay details.

If we were to continue with the other use cases, we would find that the extensions in Take Up Reservation occur in several use cases. As a convenience, we can factor this out into a separate use case:

Name   **Identify reservation**

Initiator   **Included only**

Goal   **Identify an existing reservation**

Main Success Scenario
1. Actor provides reservation tag.
2. System locates reservation.

Extensions
2. System cannot find a reservation with the given tag.
   a. Actor provides name and post code.
   b. System displays active reservations for that customer.
   c. Actor selects the reservation.
   d. Stop.
2. The reservation tag refers to a reservation at a different hotel.
   a2. Fail
2b. No active reservations at this hotel for this customer.
   a. Fail

We can then simplify the Take Up Reservation use case:

Name   **Take up reservation**

Initiator   **Guest**

Goal   **Claim a reservation and check in to the hotel**

Main Success Scenario
1. Guest arrives at hotel and claims a reservation.
2. Include Identify Reservation.
3. Guest confirms details of stay duration, room type.
4. System allocates room.
5. System notifies billing system that a stay is starting.

Extensions
3. Reservation not identified.
   a. Fail

The use case diagram can now reflect the inclusion, as in Figure 4.6.

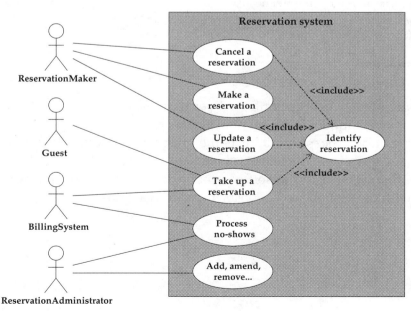

Figure 4.6 Included use case

4.4.4   Quality of Service

So far we haven't said anything about quality of service. We ought to add a quality of service section to each use case stating our expectations, especially in the areas of security and performance. Where these requirements are system-wide, we can state them separately.

For example, we might say:

> Only authorized users (identified by a password) may access the reservation service, other than via the Internet.

For the Make a Reservation use case, our quality of service statement might be

---

Make a Reservation

The system must support 200 simultaneous users.

System response to any input must not exceed 2 seconds (95 percent) for direct connections and 5 seconds (90 percent) for Internet connections.

The system must support (total number of rooms) * 10 active reservations, and assume 100 percent hotel occupancy.

4.5   Summary

The requirements workflow must deliver to the specification workflow a business concept model and a set of use cases.

The business concept model lists the important concepts in the problem domain and shows the relationships between them.

The use cases clarify the software boundary, identify the actors who interact with the system, and describe those interactions.

Chapter 5

Component Identification

Component identification, illustrated in Figure 5.1, is the first stage of the specification workflow. It leads on from the requirements workflow, taking the business concept model and the use case model as inputs.

The goal of component identification is to create an initial set of interfaces and component specifications, hooked together into a first-cut component architecture. It thus creates a backdrop for the subsequent specification

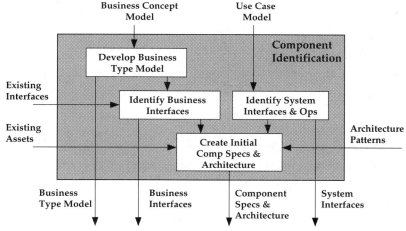

Figure 5.1   The component identification stage of the specification workflow

workflows to refine and fill in. It also produces an important internal specification workflow artifact—the business type model, which is used later to
develop interface information models. The emphasis at this stage is on
discovery—what information needs to be managed, what interfaces are
needed to manage it, what components are needed to provide that functionality, and how they will fit together.

The approach is predicated on the view we've taken of application
architecture layers, discussed in Chapter 1. There we separated the system
into two distinct layers: the system services layer and the business services
layer. This separation permeates the specification workflow. At this stage
we aim to identify the system interfaces and system components in the
system services layer, and the business interfaces and business type components in the business services layer.

In addition to the discovery of new components, we also need to take
into account existing interfaces, systems, databases, or components that
we'll need to interface with and that may need adapting. We also try to
apply architectural patterns and design criteria as appropriate.

5.1   Identifying Interfaces

This book is mostly concerned with the business system, which is the
user-interface-independent aspect of an application and corresponds to
what you might think of as the server side of things.

Consider the application architecture layers in Figure 5.2; we characterize the user dialog layer as corresponding to user dialog software,
which acts as the initiator of operations on our system interfaces. We
aren't focusing on this side of things, so we simply represent the role of
this software as one or more dialog types.

The dialog software effectively implements what we can call the use case
logic—that is, the software that handles user-system dialog according to the
specified use cases. As we've seen, we break use cases down into steps and
use those steps to identify the system operations needed to fulfil the system's
responsibilities. Use case step logic corresponds to the software dealing with
particular use case steps—the steps that have full or partial system responsi-

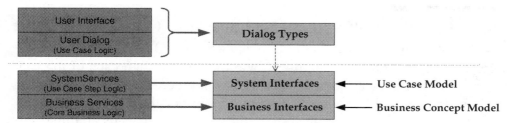

Figure 5.2 Interface inputs and correspondence to application architecture layers

bility. For a given step, the system may need to provide zero, one, or multiple operations to meet its responsibilities—this is not a one-to-one mapping.

So the system interfaces and their initial operations emerge from a consideration of the use case model. The system interfaces are focused on, and derived from, the system's interactions.

We use the business concept model to help us focus on the information and associated processes that the system will need to manage. We refine the business concept model, representing a human's-eye view of the world, into a business type model that represents the system's-eye view of the world, and then use that to develop a set of business interfaces. The implementations of components supporting these interfaces form the core business logic. The operations of the system components carry out their work by invoking operations of the business interfaces.

Here's how this all works at runtime. When the user initiates a use case, the use case logic causes the appropriate UI to be created and displayed. The user is guided through the use case steps by the use case logic. Whenever the use case logic needs information to display or needs to notify the system of a user action, it calls the appropriate operation in the use case step logic. This operation, in turn, uses operations defined in the core business logic to perform its function.

Needless to say, these layers are a guide, not mandatory boundaries. Operation invocations may also take place within a layer or may skip layers. For example, the use case dialog software may invoke a business interface operation directly. However, the invocation direction is mandatory. A component may only invoke operations in its own level or in a level below itself. It may not invoke operations of components in a level above itself.

5.2   Identifying System Interfaces and Operations

As a first-cut approach we define one dialog type and one system interface per use case as shown in Figure 5.3. We then go through each of the use cases and for each step consider whether or not there are system responsibilities that must be modeled. If so, we represent them as one or more operations of the appropriate system interface. This gives us an initial set of interfaces and operations to work from. If there are several consecutive use case steps that are all system responsibilities, these can be collapsed into a single operation—but don't do that if you think these steps might later need to be split (e.g., by an extension).

In Chapter 6 we reassess which interfaces should take responsibility for which operations, so we may find that these initial operations are moved to other interfaces.

Let's examine some of the use cases in the case study.

5.2.1   Make a Reservation

For our use case, we define an initial system interface called IMakeReservation. In the main success scenario, in step 2 we see that the system must allow the person making the reservation the ability to get details of different hotels, then for a given selection provide (in step 3) a price and availa-

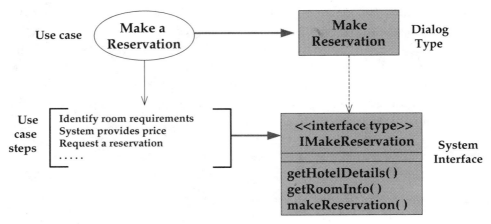

Figure 5.3   Use cases map to system interfaces

bility for a given request. We'll call these the getHotelDetails( ) and getRoomInfo( ) operations. In step 7 we can deduce the need for a make-Reservation( ) operation that creates a reservation given various details, returns a reference number, and confirms the reservation.

The use case extensions describe alternative behavior under certain situations. From the Room not available extension we can see that the user may select alternative dates or room types. But this is not an operation of the system—the display and selection of information will be handled by the user dialog logic.

5.2.2 Take Up Reservation

The next system interface we define is ITakeUpReservation. In the Take Up Reservation use case the guest arrives and checks in at the hotel. She provides a reservation reference number and the system has to identify that reservation (step 3). We'll call this the getReservation( ) operation. The details of the booking are confirmed with the guest. To commence a stay, the system allocates a room and notifies the billing system that a stay has begun. This is all handled by the beginStay( ) operation.

The two interfaces defined so far are illustrated in Figure 5.4. We haven't yet defined the parameters for the operations. We delay that until we look at the object interactions, covered in the next chapter.

The interfaces we have defined at the system services level are specific to that system and will not typically be reusable by different systems (although they will of course be used multiple times if a number of different applications is required with the same underlying system). Reuse of interfaces across systems is the purpose of the business interfaces, which should aim to be system-independent, and that's what we'll discuss next.

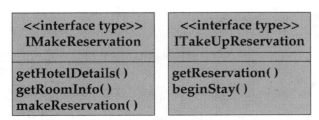

Figure 5.4   Initial system interfaces—initial operations

5.3   Identifying Business Interfaces

The business interfaces are abstractions of the information that must be managed by the system. Our process for identifying them is as follows:

1. Produce a scoped copy of the business concept model as the business type model.

2. Refine the business type model and specify any additional business rules with constraints .

3. Identify **Core Business Types**.

4. Create business interfaces for core types and add them to the business type model.

5. Refine the business type model to indicate business interface responsibilities.

This isn't quite the full story because we also need to check that the interfaces we define align with any overriding policies, such as those defined in a corporate component architecture.

5.3.1   Create the Business Type Model

The first step in identifying business types is to convert the business concept model produced by the requirements workflow into a business type model. If you're interested in traceability, the best approach is to take a copy of the business concept model. If you're sure you don't want to keep the business concept model, you can just edit it directly. We advocate retaining and maintaining the business concept model—from a project point of view it represents one of the main communication vehicles with the business. From a UML point of view the two models are related with a «trace» dependency, as shown in Figure 5.5.

The business type model is represented by a UML class diagram, like the concept model, but its purpose is different. Whereas the concept model is simply a map of the information of interest in the problem domain, the business type model contains the specific business information that must be held by the system being specified.

A business type defines the data/state that the enterprise needs to keep and monitor, and is well-recognized as a business concept or process

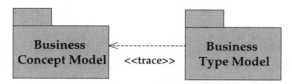

Figure 5.5 Deriving the business type model from the business concept model

by users and management. It is important to recognize that business types may correspond to nonphysical aspects of the business, such as processes, just as much as to physical artifacts of the business. For example, an order is just as much a business type as a product is. Often, forms or documents will exist which represent these nonphysical business types.

5.3.2 Refine the Business Type Model

The business type model is initially created by copying the concept model and adding or removing elements until its scope is correct. See Figure 5.6.

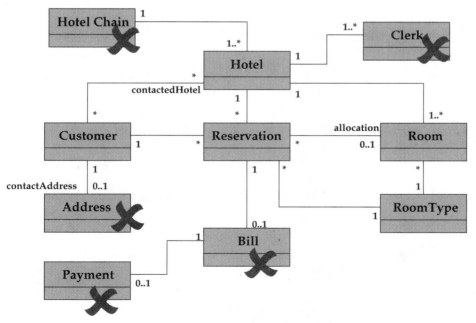

Figure 5.6 Scoping the business type model

We can eliminate the HotelChain type because the requirements call for a system that supports only a single chain of hotels. We can eliminate the Hotel-Customer association, as discussed in Chapter 4, Table 4.2. We can eliminate Payment and Bill because the reservation system does not support billing or payments; these are the domain of a separate billing system. We have also eliminated Clerk and Address to keep the example simpler.

We then further refine the model by filling in any details that have been omitted at the concept level, in particular the details of the attributes on each type, defining a set of data types for use in this model, and defining model constraints such as association multiplicities. This gives us the initial business type model shown in Figure 5.7. The business type model needs to be a precise model—it is the base from which the business interfaces will emerge.

5.3.3   Define Business Rules

Now that we have a precise base to work with, we set about adding any additional required business rules to the simple ones captured directly through association role multiplicities. This means writing some constraints and introducing new attributes. At this stage in the specification workflow, constraints are often written in natural language. We don't need to go to the effort of creating formal specifications until everything is stable or the constraint is simply stated. Formal specifications are produced at the component specification stage of the workflow.

First, we can identify which associations can be derived from others. For example, a hotel reservation must be for rooms at that same hotel, and

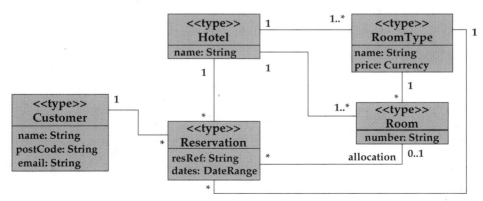

Figure 5.7 Initial business type

the type of room specified must be available at that same hotel. These constraints are added in Figure 5.8—in UML notation the constraint text is put in braces ({}), and we have written the constraint bodies in OCL.

Further, we may want to define some room pricing and availability rules, and introduce new attributes to manifest these, such as the following.

Availability Rules

- A room is available if the number of rooms reserved on all dates in the requested range is less than the number of rooms. We introduce a new parameterized attribute available( ) for RoomType on which to hang this rule. So available(theDateRange) is true if that type of room is available over theDateRange.

- You can never have more reservations for a date than rooms (no overbooking).

Pricing Rule

- The price of a room for a stay is the sum of the prices for the days in the stay. To capture this we change the price attribute on RoomType to be parameterized by date, so that we have variable pricing in our model. We introduce a new attribute, stayPrice, on which to hang this pricing rule.

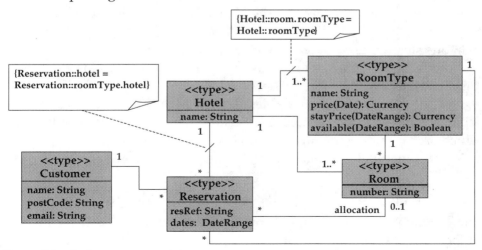

Figure 5.8 Business type model

Adding the extra attributes allows us to write these rules in OCL if we want. This gives us the updated business type model shown in Figure 5.8.

5.3.4   Identify Core Types

Next we decide which types in the business type model we consider to be core. The purpose of identifying core types is to start thinking about which information is dependent on which other information, and which information can stand alone. This is a useful step toward allocating information responsibilities to interfaces.

A core business type is a business type that has independent existence within the business, characterized by the following:

- A business identifier, usually independent of other identifiers

- Independent existence—no mandatory associations, except to a categorizing type

The second point needs a little explanation. A categorizing type is one whose instances categorize or classify the instances of another type. This is not an aggregation or composition association, simply a classifying one. For example, Room has a mandatory association with RoomType, but RoomType is a categorizing type for Room, so Room could still be a core type. We do not make Room a core type, however, since it also has a mandatory association with Hotel.

Core types are indicated in the business type model by giving them the «core» stereotype. UML doesn't allow model elements to have more than one stereotype, so «core» subsumes «type» semantics.

In our case study, we apply the rules and quickly decide that Hotel and Customer are the core types.

All the other types provide details of the core types. These detailing types are likely to be repeating or conditional collections of attributes, which are not independently tracked by the business. They have a (direct or indirect) mandatory association with one or more core types.

5.3.5   Create Business Interfaces and Assign Responsibilities

The general rule is that we create one business interface for each core type in the business type model. Each business interface manages the information represented by the core type and its detailing types. Because it typi-cally manages sets of instances of the core type, we often refer to these kinds of business interface as manager interfaces and name them IxxxMgt (e.g., ICustomerMgt, interface for Customer management).

We also consider modifying the core type itself to become an interface. This would mean that individual instances of the core type would be sep-arate component objects. At this stage we do not make that decision. The value of having component objects at the individual business instance level is investigated when we consider implementation technology map-pings in Chapter 8. At this stage, we just define manager interfaces that manage all the business instances as data structures.

The Customer type in the business type model is a good example. If we made this a business interface in its own right we would need many instances of the component that supports it, one per customer. Instead we create a manager interface called ICustomerMgt, of which there will be few instances (probably just one), and Customer becomes a data structure within that interface. A single component object supporting ICustomer-Mgt would then manage many customers.

The key effect of this change is in the way we refer to a particular cus-tomer within the software at runtime. If we had an ICustomer interface we could refer to a particular customer using a reference to a component object offering that interface. But with an ICustomerMgt interface we must refer to a particular customer using a key or identifier that is passed as a parameter to all operations of ICustomerMgt that manipulate the customer's details.

Now that we have added some initial business interfaces to the busi-ness type model, we refer to any diagrams that depict these interfaces as interface responsibility diagrams; Figure 5.9 is an example.

The purpose of these diagrams is to clarify which information will be managed by which interfaces and to start thinking through any depend-encies. To do this we allocate ownership of the detailing types to the appropriate interface. Each type should be owned by exactly one inter-face. Allocation of types to interfaces is shown by a composition associa-tion (solid diamond symbol).

If a detailing type only provides the detail for one other type, it is allo-cated to the same interface as that type. If the detailing type details more than one type but they are all allocated to the same interface, the detailing

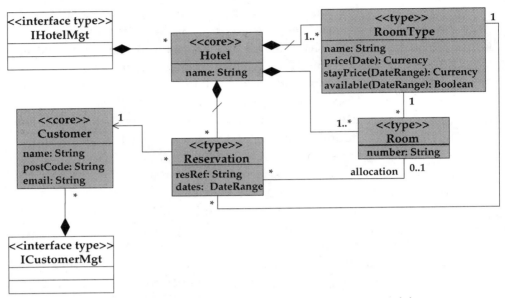

Figure 5.9   Interface responsibility diagram of the business type model

type belongs to that interface too. Where it gets tricky is when a type details other types that are allocated to different interfaces. For example, is Reservation providing details of both Hotel and Customer? Which interface takes charge of Reservation? And what do we do with Reservation's associations?

We allocate the Reservation type to IHotelMgt because it is more tightly coupled with the other information managed by IHotelMgt and it has only a simple reference to Customer. To indicate this we mark the association between Reservation and Customer to be navigable only toward Customer. (We discuss this later in this chapter). The result of all this activity is an interface responsibility diagram of the business type model, as shown in Figure 5.9.

5.3.6   Allocating Responsibility for Associations

When an association exists between types managed by different interfaces, we refer to it as an **Inter-Interface Association**. The association between Customer and Reservation is just such an association. A decision has to be made about where this information will be recorded (that is, which interface(s) will store[1] the reference(s), and where referential integrity will be maintained (i.e., which component will take responsibility for a given reference being valid). At this stage we are concerned more with where the information will be recorded. Referential integrity is considered in the context of component object architectures in Chapter 6.

One of the high-level goals we've been striving for is that of reducing dependencies—building good systems from components is primarily a dependency-management problem. Inter-interface associations can be thought of as specific form of dependency. For this reason we really want to avoid, wherever possible, two-way references between interfaces, so we assign one-way navigability to all inter-interface associations. This immediately tells us which interface is responsible for storing the reference. In our example, we decide that Reservation references Customer, and Customer is independent of Reservation, so we make the association navigable one-way in the appropriate direction (see Figure 5.10). This means IHotelMgt will be responsible for storing the reference to Customer.

This also acts as an important input into the interface specification task that focuses on the specification of a single interface. Assigning reference direction to the associations means that you are defining more precisely which information each interface has to maintain, and you can use this to develop the interface information model (see Chapter 7).

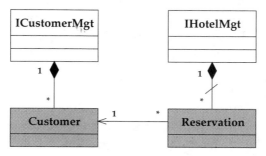

Figure 5.10   Assigning reference direction

---

1. How this is achieved in the implementation is, of course, a totally separate issue.

5.4   Creating Initial Interface Specifications

The system interfaces (and their operations) that we created earlier, which aren't part of the business type model, form an initial set of interface specifications that subsequent stages will refine directly. Right from the start we create packages in the interface specifications package to hold them.

The business type model, however, and the business interfaces we add to it when drawing the interface responsibility diagram, is an internal workflow artifact. It is a step toward our goal of creating independent business interface specifications. So, the business type model itself is not a primary deliverable of the complete specification workflow. You may therefore decide to discard it once it has fulfilled its purpose. On the other hand, you may wish to retain it (and hence maintain it) as part of the documentation of the component architecture.

Once we are happy with the interface responsibility diagram we create another set of business interfaces in the interface specifications package, each with its own subpackage, corresponding to the business interfaces we created in the business type model. We also copy into the package, for each interface, all those types in the business type model for which the interface is responsible. This gives us a good base for the interface information model of each interface. We go into this in more detail in Chapter 7.

We insert these copy steps into the process because we want to capture initial component specifications and their interfaces early, but we'll want to refine them later, and we don't want the component specifications and their interface specifications referring directly to elements in the business type model. This is because we don't want changes and refinements to these detailed specification deliverables affecting the business type model. The ongoing purpose of the business type model, should you decide to keep and maintain it, is to show an integrated view of how the information managed by the system as a whole is related—it is a single, integrated model. When we go to multiple, independent interfaces this single integrated view would otherwise be lost.

So, to recap, the system interfaces are created directly in their interface specifications folder, whereas the initial business interfaces are created in the business type model. Separate, duplicate, business interface specifica-

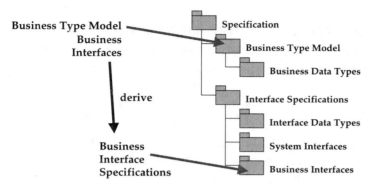

Figure 5.11 Package structure detail

tions are then created in the interface specifications folder as a base for component specification (see Figure 5.11). These can then be evolved separately. The business type model need not be retained, but we prefer to do so because it gives an integrated view.

5.5   Existing Interfaces and Systems

We have identified the system interfaces, which are derived from the use cases, and we have the initial business interfaces, which were discovered against the business type model and then copied to their own packages under the interface specifications package. We now augment the set by adding in any additional interfaces that are part of the environment into which the reservation system will be deployed. In particular, are there any existing interfaces that we are obliged to use? Are there interfaces for components that form part of an existing, broader-scoped component architecture? And are there any systems with which we need to interface, but which are outside the specific scope of this development project?

In the case study we have an existing billing system with a designated interface. This system has been in production for a number of years and we need to make use of its functionality. So we add this interface to our set of system interfaces.

5.6 Component Specification Architecture

We now create an initial set of component specifications and form an idea of how they might fit together. The component is the unit of deployment and replacement in a component system. Components are what we build or buy; they are the units of realization. Therefore we must choose components such that it makes sense to build, or buy, that unit of functionality. You can upgrade a system by replacing components selectively. Therefore we must take care to specify components such that the units of replacement are what we want and what we can manage.

There are a number of potential inputs to this activity at this stage:

- The interfaces in the interface model

- Existing component specifications that we aim to reuse

- An existing component specification architecture that we need to adapt

- A choice of component specification architecture patterns

In most cases we will create a separate component specification for each interface specification we have identified. However, we can support multiple interfaces on a single component specification in the following circumstances:

- The concepts represented by the different interfaces have the same lifetimes (i.e., they are created and deleted at the same time). This is often the case for interfaces with highly "overlapping" interface information models.

- The interactions between the interfaces are complex, frequent, or involve large amounts of data. (This is a good example of why the process is iterative—we need to come back and refine the architecture once we've examined the component interactions).

- We are happy that the implementations of the interfaces are replaced simultaneously, as a unit.

- We want to keep component granularity at a reasonable size for project management and organizational purposes.

5.6.1 System Component Specifications

In our case study, the use-case-derived system interfaces are strongly overlapping and manage concepts that have the same lifetimes. We could choose to have them supported by a single component specification. But bundling the existing Billing System in with the others makes no sense when we consider the implications for component deployment and replacement. We want to be able to build or upgrade their implementations separately. We therefore put IMakeReservation and ITakeUpReservation on one component specification, and keep IBilling separate on another component specification. The Reservation system makes use of IBilling, so we add the dependency between them. We also add in interface dependencies on ICustomerMgt and IHotelMgt, although we don't know if these really exist at this stage. We will validate these when we study the component interactions. We arrive at two separate system component specifications, as shown in Figure 5.12. We combine them into an architecture shortly.

5.6.2 Business Component Specifications

For the business interfaces, our starting point is one component specification per interface. Since the manager interfaces were created to manage instances of «core» business types and their associated details, they are, almost by definition, concerned with information that is managed independently. So,

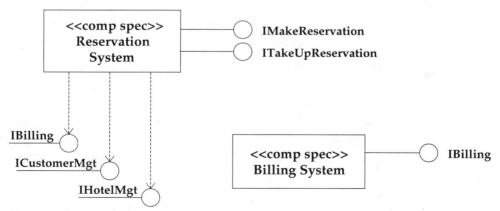

Figure 5.12 System component specifications

ICustomerMgt and IHotelMgt lead to separate component specifications, as shown in Figure 5.13.

We adopt a naming convention of naming manager interfaces IxxxMgt (where "Mgt" is short for "management"), and naming any directly corresponding component specifications xxxMgr (where "Mgr" is short for "manager").

5.6.3 An Initial Architecture

Now we have an initial set of component specifications, including their supported interfaces and their interface dependencies. Since we don't have any interfaces being offered by more than one component specification in our example, we can bind the interface dependencies of the component specifications directly onto their corresponding component specification interfaces, giving us the component specification architecture shown in Figure 5.14.

Figure 5.13 Business component specifications

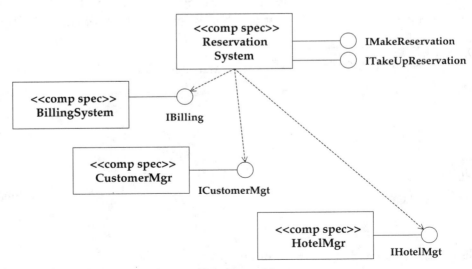

Figure 5.14 Initial component specification architecture

5.7 Summary

We have produced an initial set of system interface specifications, business interface specifications, and component specifications, and we have formed an initial component architecture. We have also created a business type model that contains a rich set of type information and business rules. This is the raw material from which the interface specifications are built. Some of the main principles are as follows:

- The system interfaces correspond to use cases, and their operations are derived from use case steps.

- A business type model is developed representing the system's-eye view of the business concept model. Business rules are captured on the business type model as constraints. The business type model is an internal workflow artifact, which is useful to maintain.

- Business interfaces are discovered by identifying core types in the business type model and creating interfaces to manage them and their details.

- Initial business interface specifications are created by copying the business type model business interfaces, and their view of the business type model (the types for which they are responsible) into separate interface packages. At this point the integrated model we started with is split apart into independently evolving models. These interface specifications are refined in subsequent stages.

- Initial component specifications are defined and formed into an initial component architecture. Existing systems and architectures are taken into account.

At this stage we have simply laid out the structural ground to enable the component interactions to be investigated. That's what we'll look at next.

Chapter 6

Component Interaction

The component identification activities described in Chapter 5 give us an initial set of interfaces and components with which to work. Now we will decide how the components will work together to deliver the required functionality. We call this second stage of the specification workflow, illustrated in Figure 6.1, **Component Interaction**.

Interaction modeling is a generic behavioral modeling technique. We use it here to define the various interactions that need to take place inside

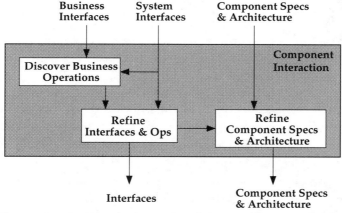

Figure 6.1 The component interaction stage of the specification workflow

the system, to refine existing interface definitions, to identify how interfaces will be used, and to discover new interfaces and operations. Since it encompasses the assessment of multiple interactions, it also involves spotting common patterns of usage, identifying general operations to replace specific ones, and understanding interface dependencies. All this, in turn, forces us to re-examine and refine the component architecture.

As we explained in Chapter 3, we use UML collaboration diagrams to model interactions. Our collaboration diagrams depict component objects that support particular interfaces. Each box is like an instance of an interface. You may be more familiar with the use of UML interaction diagrams to model object-oriented programming language class objects, representing the implementation design of a particular operation. We're applying the same ideas to the specification of an interaction, rather than the implementation. We're defining the implementation constraints—the rules that must hold for *all* implementations of these components. The alert reader may have noticed a recurring theme here.

6.1   Discovering Business Operations

Figure 6.2 shows the component architecture we created in the previous chapter. We also identified the operations required on two system interfaces:

```
IMakeReservation
getHotelDetails()
getRoomInfo()
makeReservation()

ITakeUpReservation
getReservation()
beginStay()
```

We don't know the signatures of these operations at this point, nor how they will be implemented using the business components. What's more, we haven't yet identified the operations needed on the business interfaces.

It's important to keep in mind that we are trying to produce a specification, not an implementation design, and we must be careful to avoid over-specification. Our component architecture diagram already tells implementers of ReservationSystem that they must use the ICustomerMgt and IHotelMgt interfaces. We may not want to place any further constraints

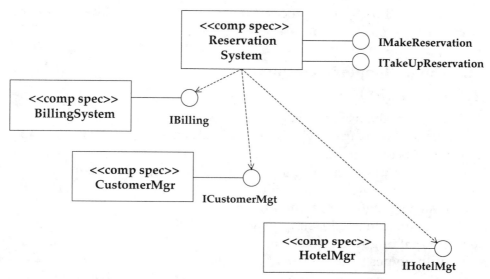

Figure 6.2 Initial component architecture

on the precise way in which implementations of ReservationSystem must use these interfaces. That's fine, but we don't yet have any operations defined on the business interfaces.

Of course, we could just let the component implementers decide on the contents of the interface, but then the exact nature of those operations would be a matter of negotiation between the component implementers, rather than a broader architectural decision. Therefore we believe it is important that you follow the process described in this chapter to discover the appropriate business interface operations, even if you subsequently decide not to place rigid constraints on their use.

To discover the business interface operations we take each system interface operation in turn and draw one or more collaboration diagrams that trace any constraints on flows of execution resulting from an invocation of that operation. Each collaboration diagram should show one or more interactions, where each interaction shows one possible execution flow. So if there are several important alternative flows you will need to draw several interactions.

Let's walk through that process for some of the system interface operations identified so far in our case study.

6.1.1   Some Simple Interactions

getHotelDetails( )

We know from the use case that the purpose of getHotelDetails( ) is to provide a list of hotels from which the user can choose. Rather than simply return details of all the hotels, we decide the user must supply a string to be used as a partial match against the hotel names; only details of hotels with matching names will be returned. We don't need to worry about the exact matching algorithm right now.

The operation could simply return a list of hotel names, but we decide that it ought to return a unique hotel identifier for each hotel and a list of the types of room each hotel has. Why do we make these decisions? We use hotel identifiers primarily because the names of hotels might not be unique.[1] We return room types because we know that later in the use case we will need them. We could introduce another operation to fetch the room types for a particular hotel, which we would call once the user has made his or her selection, but we need to trade off the overhead of making this extra call with the overhead of returning the extra data in the getHotelDetails( ) call.

So there is a fair bit of information to return for each matching hotel and the operation will be returning potentially many such sets of information. In these circumstances it is best to define a structured data type to hold the information for each hotel. We called it HotelDetails (see Figure 6.3). We will return a collection of these structures. HotelId is a new scalar data type we have introduced to represent hotel identifiers—you can imagine it being an integer or perhaps a string.

The signature of this operation becomes

```
IMakeReservation::getHotelDetails(in match:String):HotelDetails [ ]
```

---

1. In this simple example a user wouldn't be able to distinguish between two hotels with the same name, but we could easily extend the case study to add hotel locations and addresses.

```
        <<data type>>
         HotelDetails
  ──────────────────────────
  id: HotelId
  name: String
  roomTypes: String [ ]
```

Figure 6.3 Structured data type for hotel details

We pass in a string to match with hotel names, and we return a collection of HotelDetails. We can now refine our definition of the IMakeReservation interface by adding the details of the operation signature.

At runtime, this operation is invoked by the dialog layer on a ReservationSystem component object. That object is not able to satisfy the operation itself because system components don't store business data, so it must use a component object offering the IHotelMgt interface. The required interaction is shown in Figure 6.4.

As shown in Figure 6.4, we decide that IHotelMgt should also have a getHotelDetails() operation, with the same signature. The ReservationSystem object simply passes the call through.

As explained in Chapter 3, the UML naming rules for roles in a collaboration are objectname/rolename:classifiername. We're using anonymous objects, so they are unnamed. Because the ReservationSystem only has knowledge of a single set of business component objects (see Figure 6.9), they don't need naming. We use the role name to indicate the interface of the object we are dealing with, and the component specification name follows the

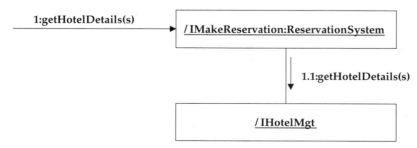

Figure 6.4 getHotelDetails( )

colon. We also show the operation arguments (parameter instances), which is useful for seeing how the information is passed around and for writing any conditions or constraints based on their values.

We haven't shown the component specification name of the object offering IHotelMgt because it isn't necessary—the object only receives messages in this interaction. If it also sent a message this would be an implementation constraint and we would have to call out the component specification on which we wanted to define such a constraint.[2]

We have discovered our first business interface operation. We should now update the definition of IHotelMgt to add the operation.

getRoomInfo( )

We deal with getRoomInfo( ) in a very similar way. The operation must be supplied with the selected hotel identifier, the dates for the proposed stay, and the required room type. It must return availability and price.

Once again, we define a structured data type to hold information about the proposed reservation, as shown in Figure 6.5. We have used another new data type here, DateRange, defined by two dates, the starting date and the ending date.

```
<<data type>>
ReservationDetails

hotel: HotelId
dates:  DateRange
roomType: String
```

Figure 6.5   Structured data type for reservation details

---

2. If we did not name the invoking component specification, we would in fact be defining a very stringent constraint that *all* components implementing that interface had to make such an invocation. There are situations where this can be useful, such as in the specification of infrastructure services, but we do not cover them in this book.

We decide the signature for getRoomInfo( ) should be

```
IMakeReservation::getRoomInfo(
         in res: ReservationDetails,
         out availability: Boolean,
         out price: Currency)
```

As with getHotelDetails( ), we decide that the ReservationSystem object should simply forward this call to the object offering IHotelMgt. The resulting interaction is shown in Figure 6.6.

6.1.2 Breaking Dependencies

Now it's time to look at a more interesting interaction.

makeReservation( )

The makeReservation( ) operation must create the reservation and notify the customer by e-mail. We start, as usual, by defining the signature for the operation. The operation needs to know the required reservation, so we provide a ReservationDetails structure as a parameter. It also needs to know about the customer, so we define a new structured data type to hold customer details (Figure 6.7). This structure holds the name of the customer and has two optional attributes to hold the customer's post code and e-mail address. If this is a new customer all three attributes are required, but if this is an existing customer the post code is required only if the name isn't unique, and the e-mail address isn't ever required because we already have it (but the customer might supply it anyway).

Figure 6.6   getRoomInfo() interaction

<<data type>> CustomerDetails
name: String postCode[0..1]: String email[0..1]: String

Figure 6.7   Structured data type for reservation details

We know from the use case that the system must return a tag or reference number for the newly created reservation. We use a string for this, so that we can deal with alphanumeric references. The signature of the operation becomes

```
IMakeReservation::makeReservation(
        in res: ReservationDetails,
        in cus: CustomerDetails,
        out resRef: String): Integer
```

Why does it return an integer? Well, things can go wrong. We are using the return value to indicate the outcome of the operation, as follows:

0   Success.

1   This is not an existing customer and the system was not able to create a new record because the post code and/or e-mail address were not provided.

2   No post code was provided and the name matches more than one customer.

An alternative would have been for the operation to return a more complex structure with more information, or to raise exceptions, but we'll keep things simple for the moment.

Internally (i.e., within the system) we refer to a customer using a customer identifer (CustId), much as we did with hotels. The difference is that while we are happy to pass hotel identifiers to the dialog layer we will keep customer identifiers as an internal concept only. CustId will never appear in the signature of a system interface operation.

We need an operation on ICustomerMgt to look up a customer's details and return his or her CustId, so we invent one:

```
ICustomerMgt::getCustomerMatching(
            in custD: CustomerDetails,
            out cusId: CustId): Integer
```

Here, the return values are

0   Success—a single customer matched and his or her identifier is returned.

1   This is not an existing customer.

2   No post code was provided and the name matches more than one customer.

Which of our components is going to call that operation?

We made an important decision in Chapter 5: The HotelMgr component is responsible for storing the association between reservations and customers. But we also made another important but less obvious decision, reflected in the component specification architecture: The HotelMgr component and the CustomerMgr component are independent of each other. We can't just let the ReservationSystem component forward the makeReservation() call to the HotelMgr and let it get on with it, because the HotelMgr would then have to use ICustomerMgt to check the customer details. Instead, the ReservationSystem is going to have to do this.

Figure 6.8 shows the resulting interaction, for the case where details of the customer are already on file. The ReservationSystem finds the customer's identifier, then passes it in the call to IHotelMgt so that it can be stored against that reservation. The returned reservation reference is passed back to the dialog layer once the customer has been notified. We decide that the notifyCustomer() operation will take as parameters the customer's identifier and a string containing the message we want to send. You can find the full signatures of the operations later in the chapter in Figures 6.14 and 6.15.

It seems a minor detail, but by using customer identifiers, and by having ReservationSystem deal with converting the customer's details into an identifier, we have ensured that the HotelMgr and CustomerMgr components are free from interdependencies. This helps make these components more reusable in other contexts. ReservationSystem is providing the usage context.

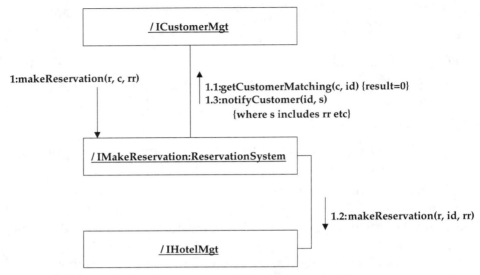

Figure 6.8   makeReservation( ) interaction (existing customer)

What we can see emerging here is a clearer understanding of the responsibility of each interface and component, and the dependencies between them. IMakeReservation delegates reservations to IHotelMgt and manages the association with the customer. IHotelMgt is responsible for rooms and types of room, reservations against those room types, and the room pricing. ICustomerMgt is responsible for keeping track of customers and their details, and handling customer notification.

6.2   Maintaining Referential Integrity

6.2.1   Component Object Architecture

Although we know from our component specification architecture that certain kinds of components will exist, we haven't said how many component objects of each kind we will have at runtime.

You might have assumed—reasonably enough—that there will be one ReservationSystem component object of each kind. But imagine if that were not true; imagine two CustomerMgr component objects, each with its own set of customers, and no guarantee of globally unique customer identities. If the ReservationSystem skipped between use of these two, confusion would reign.

We need to say clearly that the ReservationSystem will always use the same business component objects. We can do that using a component specification diagram for the ReservationSystem component. Since this is a UML class diagram, we can define associations between the component specification and the interfaces it uses (Figure 6.9). We can then define multiplicity constraints on those associations. Figure 6.9 makes it clear that ReservationSystem will always use the same objects for hotel management, customer management, and billing. This diagram is strictly part of the component specification for ReservationSystem, and we explain it more fully in Chapter 7.

6.2.2 Controlling Intercomponent References

As we saw earlier in this chapter, the HotelMgr component object holds the identities of customers as part of the reservation information. How can we ensure that these identities are always valid? What happens if we delete a customer?

In general, there are a number of options for allocating responsibility for ensuring that intercomponent references are valid. These can also be used in combination.

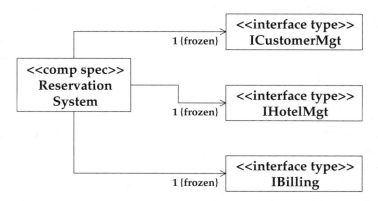

Figure 6.9 Constraints on the component object architecture

1. Responsibility can be allocated to the component object storing the reference—give it total and exclusive responsibility. In our example this would mean making sure that all requests to delete customers are sent to the HotelMgr component object; it would then be responsible for passing the request to its CustomerMgr component object. No other component object would be able to access this CustomerMgr component object.

2. Responsibility can be allocated to the component object that owns the target of the reference. In our example this would be CustomerMgr. It would have to have a mechanism for knowing which other components are holding references to it and notifying them appropriately.

3. Responsibility can be given to a third component object, usually higher up the call chain. This would mean making the ReservationSystem responsible for customer deletions and having it interact with CustomerMgr and HotelMgr.

4. Permit, and tolerate, references to become invalid.

5. Disallow the deletion of information.

Option 1 doesn't fit with our chosen dependencies, so we discount this option. We decide that in our system we will seek to ensure that the customer references held by HotelMgr are always valid. This rules out option 4. Let's also assume that we know from the use cases that option 5 is not possible. This leaves options 2 or 3. Option 3 is the simplest. The delete request would go to ReservationSystem and it would ensure that all reservations for the customer are removed. A possible interaction for this is shown in Figure 6.10.

Unfortunately, there is a snag with option 3. It assumes that the CustomerMgr component object is exclusive to ReservationSystem and not shared with any other system. It assumes that the deleteCustomer() operation of ICustomerMgt will not be invoked from anywhere except the ReservationSystem.

As a general goal when developing systems from components, we *are* trying to reuse component objects between systems. We want to share code and data together, not just code. The creation of exclusive informa-

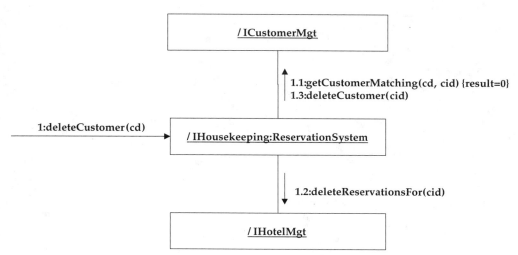

Figure 6.10   Interaction for referential integrity option 3

tion sets in different systems will reduce the integration of the business. The existence within a single business of multiple sets of customers and their details is notorious and lamentable.

However, if we can't assume exclusive assess to the CustomerMgr object we must use option 2. That is going to be more complicated because any component object holding a customer identity will have to notify the CustomerMgr component objects, which is going to have to keep a list of these dependents and notify them when deleting a customer. You might recognize this as a well-known design pattern called Observer [Gamma95].

6.3   Completing the Picture

Three further interactions complete the coverage of the use cases we've considered so far.

First, we need to examine what happens if a *new* customer makes a reservation (see Figure 6.11). This indicates the need for an operation on ICustomerMgt to create a customer.

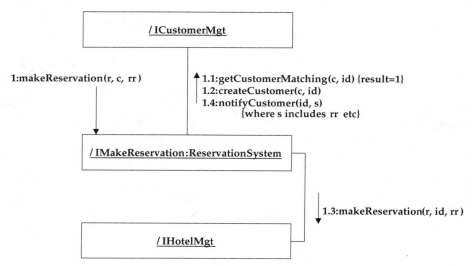

Figure 6.11   makeReservation( ) interaction (new customer)

Moving on to the Take Up Reservation use case, the getReservation( ) operation needs to return details about the reservation and the customer. Further operations on IHotelMgt and ICustomerMgt are required (see Figure 6.12). The operation returns a false result if the reservation is not found. The beginStay( ) operation needs to return the number of the allocated room and send the customer and reservation details to the billing system (see Figure 6.13). The operation returns a false result if a room cannot be allocated.

Full details of the operation signatures for the system and business interfaces are shown in Figure 6.14 and Figure 6.15.

6.4   Refining the Interfaces

During interaction modeling we've concentrated mainly on responsibility allocation and operation discovery. We haven't worried unduly about minimization of calls, cyclic dependencies, normalization of operations and interfaces, using existing design patterns, and so on. All of these things do need to be taken into account, but it's usually a good principle to

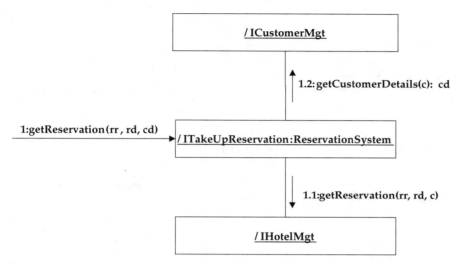

Figure 6.12 getReservation() interaction

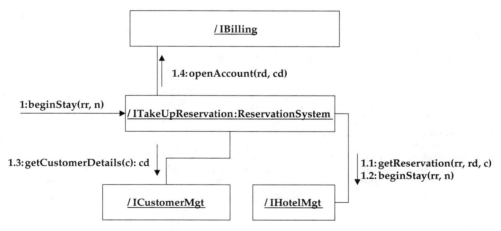

Figure 6.13 beginStay() interaction

try to do one thing at a time to avoid second guessing the best approach. We recommend that the discovery process be reasonably unfettered in its initial phase. Afterward we can bring in all these other factors to modify the specifications.

<<interface type>> IMakeReservation
getHotelDetails(in match: String): HotelDetails [ ] getRoomInfo(in res : ReservationDetails, out availability: Boolean, out price: Currency) makeReservation(in res : ReservationDetails, in cus: CustomerDetails, out resRef: String): Integer

<<interface type>> ITakeUpReservation
getReservation(in resRef: String, out rd: ReservationDetails, out cus: CustomerDetails): Boolean beginStay(in resRef: String, out roomNumber: String): Boolean

<<interface type>> IBilling
openAccount(in res : ReservationDetails, in cus: CustomerDetails)

Figure 6.14 System interfaces with operation signatures

<<interface type>> IHotelMgt
getHotelDetails(in match: String): HotelDetails [ ] getRoomInfo(in res: ReservationDetails, out availability: Boolean, out price: Currency) makeReservation(in res: ReservationDetails, in cus: CustId , out resRef: String): Boolean getReservation(in resRef: String, out rd: ReservationDetails, out cusId: CustId): Boolean beginStay(resRef: String, out roomNumbe: String): Boolean

<<interface type>> ICustomerMgt
getCustomerMatching(in custD: CustomerDetails, out cusId : CustId): Integer createCustomer(in custD: CustomerDetails, out cusId: CustId): Boolean getCustomerDetails(in cus: CustId): CustomerDetails notifyCustomer(in cus: CustId, in msg: String)

Figure 6.15 Business interfaces with operation signatures

6.4.1 Factoring Interfaces and Operations

Factoring an interface involves partitioning its responsibilities among two or more interfaces. These may be subtypes, supertypes, or peers. The goal is very similar to that of subtyping—to separate general behavior from more specialized behavior. Factoring also applies to operations in the sense that we can seek generality and nonredundancy in interface operations where appropriate. You might call this "operation normalization."

Take care not to over generalize, though. Several clear, well-scoped operations are better than one opaque one with confusing semantics and many optional parameters. Remember too that this is the world of specification. A variety of optimizations and shortcuts can be taken inside the implementation. There's usually little value in confronting the client of an interface with this complexity.

You should also seek to design for today. Don't try to anticipate future requirements by building in extra capacity and making your interfaces more general than they need to be for the known requirements. You'll invariably be wrong. Much of the flexibility in component-based system design comes from the fact that components may offer multiple interfaces. When new requirements appear, support can be provided by adding on new interfaces, and this is a better approach to dependency management than one-size-fits-all super interfaces.

6.5 Summary

We've explored a number of system interface operations, developed some interactions for them, and discovered all sorts of operations on the underlying business interfaces. We've also been consolidating our understanding of the responsibilities of each interface—what each knows about and what it doesn't.

Here is a summary of the key themes of the approach:

- Develop interaction models for each system interface operation.
- Discover business interface operations and their signatures.
- Refine responsibilities as you go.

- Define any component object architecture constraints you need.
- Factor interfaces as appropriate.

The final stage of specification is to be precise about the usage and realization contracts. This means looking at interfaces and component specifications individually and adding more detail and rigor. That's what we'll do in the next chapter.

Chapter 7

Component Specification

In Chapter 1 we examined the principles behind designing software by contract and looked at two contracts in component systems: the usage contract and the realization contract. In this chapter we define precisely how those contracts are specified.

A usage contract is defined by an interface specification. In this chapter we explore what makes up an interface and examine its various parts—sometimes in excruciating detail. If you're the type of person who likes to check the small print on your travel insurance then you'll enjoy this chapter.

A realization contract is defined by a component specification. In fact, interface specifications lie at the heart of both contracts, since component specifications are primarily groupings of interfaces. But component specifications can also contain constraints on the way the interfaces are to be implemented.

Component (and interface) specification is the final stage of the specification workflow. The activities of this stage are shown in Figure 7.1.

7.1 Specifying Interfaces

An interface is a set of operations. Each operation defines some service or function that the component object will perform for the client. An operation

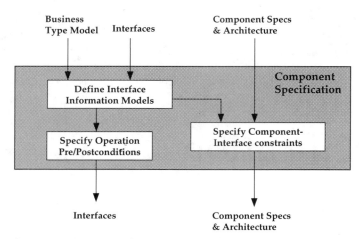

Figure 7.1 The component specification stage of the specification workflow

therefore represents a fine-grained contract between a client and a component object.

We might ask why we need an interface to be the atomic contractual unit. Why not make an operation the atomic unit? The answer is that, in general, the operation doesn't provide the right level of dependency management. This was a key objective we defined at the beginning of the book—we are trying to manage dependencies between components. But component dependencies are too specific to a particular architecture. Operation dependencies are too fine grained. Interface dependencies are just right.

For one thing, we need a construct that describes the state of a component object. Operations don't have any structural aspects to them; interfaces do. Further, interfaces group operations that belong together. This means that if a client uses one operation of an interface, it is quite likely that it will use some of the other operations, too. Sets of such operations naturally belong together and have related effects on the state of the component object. Interface factoring, which we discuss later, explicitly considers whether the operation groupings are the best for the problem in hand and for the broader architecture. Sometimes it is useful to split one interface into two or more interfaces that can be managed and evolved separately. Sometimes we want to distinguish general behavior from specializations of that behavior, so we introduce some subtyping. And sometimes an individual operation genuinely stands alone. In this case we give it an interface all to itself, to give a type to objects with that operation and to keep things consistent.

7.1.1 Operation Specification

An operation specifies an individual action that a component object will perform for a client. This has a number of facets:

- The input parameters: specifying the information provided or passed to the component object
- The output parameters: specifying the information updated or returned by the component object
- Any resulting change of state of the component object
- Any constraints that apply

The operation has to specify how the inputs, outputs, and component object state are related, and what the effect of calling the operation has on that relationship. You will recall, though, that operation specifications on interfaces do not include information about interactions between the component object performing the operation and other component objects that are required, in a specific implementation, to complete the operation. The client of the operation is unaware of such interactions.

7.1.2 Interface Information Models

We need to represent the state of the component object on which the interface depends. To do this, each interface has an interface information model. This is a type model, drawn in the interface specification diagram, of the possible states of the component object to which the operation specifications can refer. All changes to the state of the component object caused by a given operation can be described in terms of this information model definition.

The interface information model needs to contain just enough to allow the interface's operations to be specified. It's possible to build up the interface information model incrementally as you create the operation specifications, adding types, attributes, and associations as needed. In Chapter 6 we determined a need for four operations of the ICustomerMgt interface of the case study. We can study those operations to see what we need in the interface information model for that interface.

It is immediately clear that any component object offering ICustomerMgt must be holding information about customers. For each customer there are several pieces of information needed, as indicated by the CustomerDetails data type. On this evidence alone we can deduce the need for the information model shown in Figure 7.2 (we've included the definition of the CustomerDetails data type, too).

You will recall from Chapter 3 that the Customer type is an **Information Type**. An interface can only be associated with information types, and those types cannot have associations to anything outside the interface information model.[1]

Remember, this is a type model, so it is at the specification level—it specifies the set of states the component object may have. It does *not* describe the way in which that state is implemented or persisted. It is the

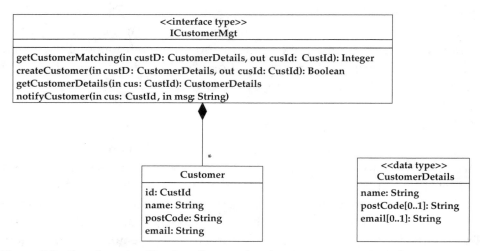

Figure 7.2   Interface specification diagram for the ICustomerMgt interface

---

1. There is an exception to this rule: An interface information model can refer to other interfaces under certain circumstances. We discuss this in Chapter 8.

view from the outside and exists purely to support the definition of constraints and the effects of operations on the state of the component object.

The set of types that form the interface information model for an interface live in a package with the interface. They are not shared with other interfaces.[2] On the other hand, data types used in the operation signatures usually live in a separate package and are imported (used) by all the interfaces that need them.

7.1.3   Pre- and Postconditions

Each operation has a pre- and a postcondition. These specify the effect of the operation without prescribing an algorithm or implementation. They act like the small print of the contract with the client. They specify in fine detail what the operation will do, and they always come as a pair. The postcondition specifies what the effect of the operation will be, provided the precondition is true.

The meaning of the precondition in UML needs emphasizing since it is often misinterpreted, especially by those used to rule-based systems and formal activity-dependency diagrams. The precondition is *not* the condition under which the operation will be called. Invocation of the operation is totally independent of the value of this condition. The precondition is the condition under which the operation guarantees that the postcondition will be true. If the precondition is false when the operation is invoked, the result is simply not specified—no assumptions about the effects of the operation can be made.

Another way of describing the precondition and postcondition is as the assumptions and guarantees of the operation. The precondition represents the assumptions that the operation is relying on for correct (i.e., well-defined) functioning. The postcondition represents the contractual guarantees that the operation makes if those assumptions are well-founded.

An important implication of viewing the operation specification in this contractual way is that the assumptions are the responsibility of the client

---

2. Except by virtue of inheritance: If one interface is a specialization of another it inherits the information model of the super-type.

of the operation, whereas the guarantees are the responsibility of the supplier of the operation (i.e., the implementation itself).

For example, a valet parking contract may guarantee that a valet will park your car for you, and will definitely guarantee to charge you, on the assumption that you leave the keys in the car. It is your responsibility to ensure the keys are there. If they are not, the valet parking behavior is unspecified. On the other hand, since most car-towing contracts cover cases where keys are unavailable, their behavior will be well-defined.

In UML these contractual conditions can be specified precisely using OCL. OCL is a declarative language that allows you to construct logical expressions. It takes awhile to get the hang of it, and writing expressions can sometimes be hard work. Even reading them can be hard work! But the payback is that the expressions have an unambiguous interpretation, not something you can claim for natural language.

As a simple example, let's consider an operation to change a customer's name (no such operation has been discussed as yet, but we might expect to need one). The specification, written in OCL, might look like this:

```
context ICustomerMgt::changeCustomerName (in cus: CustId, newName: String)
pre:
      -- cus is a valid customer id
      customer->exists(c | c.id = cus)

post:
      -- the name of the customer whose id is cus is newName
      customer->exists(c | c.id = cus and c.name = newName)
```

Just look at the comments for the moment. The postcondition comment tells you that after this operation the name of the customer whose identifier was passed as the parameter will be the string that is the other parameter. The precondition comment tells you that the postcondition is guaranteed only if a valid identifier is supplied. The OCL expressions say the same things more precisely by asserting the existence of a customer structure with the right attribute values—the term "customer" refers to the set of customers associated with (a component-object-supporting) ICustomerMgt, and the term "exists" identifies a particular member of that set.

Remember, though, that the postcondition is guaranteed only if the precondition is true. So if you call this operation and supply an invalid customer identifier, the contract doesn't hold and you can't expect anything sensible to happen.

A specification for ICustomerMgt's getCustomerDetails() operation might look like this:

```
context ICustomerMgt::getCustomerDetails (in cus: CustId): CustomerDetails

pre:
        -- cus is a valid customer id
        customer->exists(c | c.id = cus)

post:
        -- the details returned match the details of the customer
        -- whose id is cus
        -- find the customer
        Let theCust = customer->select(c | c.id = cus) in
                -- specify the result
                result.name = theCust.name and
                result.postCode = theCust.postCode and
                result.email = theCust.email
```

Invoking this operation doesn't change the state of the object that is performing it, so the postcondition is concerned only with specifying the result returned. The postcondition comment tells you that this operation will return the details of the customer whose identifier was passed as the parameter. The special OCL keyword for postconditions, "result," indicates the return value from the operation. In our example, "result" is of type CustomerDetails.

Describing how to use OCL for writing preconditions and postconditions could easily fill a book in itself, so we won't attempt to give all the details here. We'll just show examples for the operations we've defined in the case study. For a good overview of OCL we recommend Warmer and Kleppe, *The Object Constraint Language* [Warmer99]. For a full analysis of pre- and postcondition writing, we recommend *Objects, Components, and Frameworks with UML*, by D'Souza and Wills [D'Souza99].

Although we don't have space in this book to cover OCL in detail, we should explain the rules we follow for what OCL expressions in pre- and postconditions can and cannot refer to:

- The OCL expressions can refer to the operation parameters, the operation result, and the state of the component object (as defined by the interface information model).

- The OCL expressions cannot refer to anything else. In particular they cannot refer to features of any other interfaces, even if the component spec offering the interface being specified has associations with these other interfaces. Interface specifications define local effects only, where *local* means "this interface information model."

For postconditions only, expressions can refer to both the state of the component object before the operation (@pre in OCL) and its state afterward. This allows you to write expressions that specify how an attribute or association has changed as a result of the operation.

Software tools can do useful things with OCL, but it's hard going for mere mortals, notwithstanding the fact that OCL is a lot simpler to read than other formal languages. For this reason it's always worth including natural language text comments to clarify everything but the simplest OCL expression. A useful technique is to sketch out the natural language first, then define the formal OCL, then go back and modify the natural language to be more precise and to correspond to the OCL. Even if you don't fancy writing the OCL, it's always worth writing the natural language.

Writing things out formally might be harder work, and you certainly wouldn't do it until your interface definitions had become very stable, but someone, at some point, has to specify precisely what happens and under what conditions. If you omit these decisions at specification time, the component implementer will take the decisions on your behalf. And the component tester will have no clear basis for testing the component. And if you're buying the component, not building it—wouldn't you be happier with a precise specification than without one?

7.2 A Systematic Process

For complex components, creating the interface information model as a by-product of operation specification is not an effective approach.

7.2.1   From Business Type Model to Interface Information Model

In fact, we can take a shortcut in producing first-cuts of interface information models: They can be derived in a straightforward way from the business type model.

Let's return to our case study to see how this works. The interface responsibility diagram we produced in Chapter 5 is shown in Figure 7.3.

We have already decided that IHotelMgt concerns itself with hotels and reservations against rooms in those hotels. ICustomerMgt concerns itself with managing customers. The Hotel, RoomType, Room, and Reservation types have been marked as responsibilities of IHotelMgt, while the Customer type is the responsibility of ICustomerMgt. We have also decided that IHotelMgt is responsible for storing the relationship between reservations and customers, as indicated by the navigability arrow on the diagram. So it isn't a surprise that the interface information model we created for ICustomerMgt contains a Customer type.

We can use the interface responsibility diagram to deduce a first-cut interface information model for IHotelMgt. The interface information

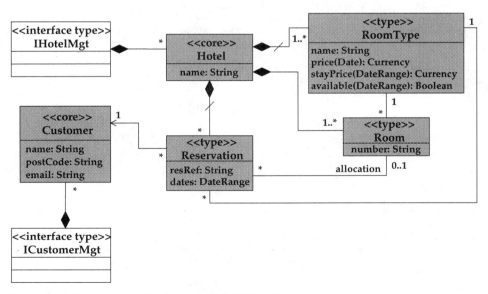

Figure 7.3   Case study interface responsibility diagram

model will clearly need to contain types for Hotel, RoomType, Room, and Reservation. But what about the Reservation-Customer association?

The rule here is simple: When a type owned by one interface refers to a type owned by another, the referenced type (Customer, in this case) appears in the interface information models of both interfaces. So there will be a Customer type in the interface information model of IHotelMgt. But it won't look the same as the Customer type in ICustomerMgt because IHotelMgt doesn't care about the customer's details—all it cares about is the identity of the customer. So the Customer type in IHotelMgt will have a single attribute: the customer identity.

The full interface information model for IHotelMgt is shown in Figure 7.4. We've added a direct association from the interface to Reservation, converted the derived association between Hotel and Reservation into a

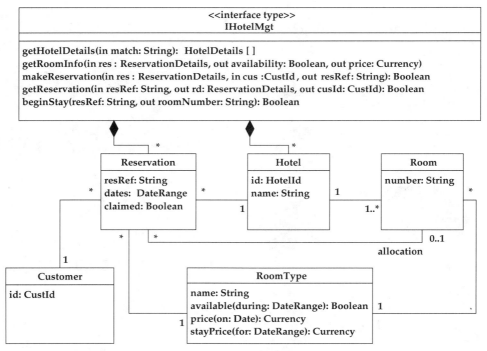

Figure 7.4 Interface specification diagram for IHotelMgt

regular association, dropped the derived association between Hotel and RoomType, and added a new attribute for Reservation (the claimed attribute). These changes are purely to simplify the specification of the operations.

Remember that the information types of an interface information model live in their own package, together with the interface itself. So there will be a type called Customer in both the IHotelMgt package and the ICustomerMgt package. These two types are separate and distinct, although they both can be traced back to the Customer type of the business type model.

A practical way of creating the interface information model for a business interface is to start by making a copy of the business type model in the interface's package, then deleting types, associations, and attributes that are not needed. You can also insert «trace» dependencies between interface information model types and business type model types if you wish, and if your tool supports the maintenance of these.

7.2.2   Invariants

An invariant is a constraint attached to a type that must be held true for all instances of the type. Many invariants can be expressed graphically, using the UML notation. For example, in Figure 7.4 the multiplicity indicator on the association between Reservation and Customer tells us there is an invariant that requires every Reservation to be associated with a single Customer.

In some cases it isn't possible or convenient to use the graphical notation. For these cases you can write the invariant in natural language—or in OCL. The following invariant relates the claimed attribute of a Reservation to the association between Reservation and Room:

```
context r : Reservation inv:
      -- a reservation is claimed if it has a room allocated to it
      r.claimed = r.allocation->notEmpty
```

With this definition in place we can use "claimed" as a shorthand, making other OCL expressions simpler to read and understand.

You might think this feels like a derived attribute, but derivation is really an implementation concept. Since this is the specification world we are simply stating an invariant linking different pieces of specification information. Having redundancy in a specification is fine if the benefits of simplicity outweigh the effort of keeping it consistent. How the implementation realizes these invariants is a totally separate question.

7.2.3 Snapshots

A useful technique when writing pre- and postconditions is to draw "before" and "after" instance diagrams and to highlight the state changes that occur. These instance diagrams are referred to as **Snapshots** in Catalysis. The instance diagrams should conform to your interface information model. If they don't, something's wrong somewhere.

Let's look at the makeReservation operation of IHotelMgt:

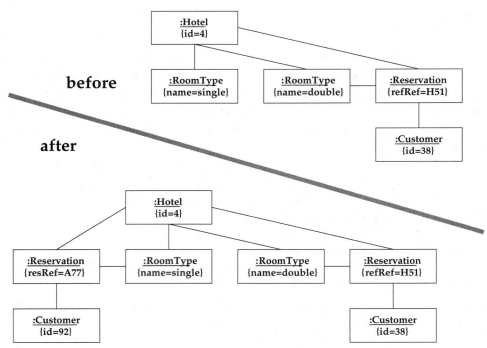

Figure 7.5 "Before" and "after" snapshot instance diagrams for IHotelMgt::makeReservation()

```
IHotelMgt::makeReservation (
      in res: ReservationDetails,
      in cus: CustId,
      out resRef: String): Boolean
```

What do we expect this operation to do? It takes some reservation details and a customer identifier and creates a new reservation.

Let's assume we invoke this operation with the following values:

```
hotel id = 4
customer id = 92
room type = single
```

Let's also assume that the hotel already has one reservation of a double room for customer 38.

Using the interface information model, we can draw simple "before" and "after" instance diagrams or snapshots to help clarify the state change (see Figure 7.5). This helps us to write the pre- and postconditions for makeReservation( ). The "before" state helps us to define the precondition, and the "after" state helps us to define the postcondition.

Here's the full operation specification:

```
context IHotelMgt::makeReservation (
    in res: ReservationDetails,
    in cus: CustId,
    out resRef: String): Boolean
pre:
    -- the hotel id and room type are valid
    hotel->exists(h | h.id = res.hotel and
        h.room.roomType.name->includes(res.roomType))
post:
    -- return value of true implies success
    result implies
        -- a reservation was created
        -- identify the hotel
        Let h = hotel->select(x | x.id = res.hotel)->asSequence->first in
            -- only one more reservation now than before
            (h.reservation - h.reservation@pre)->size = 1 and
            -- identify the reservation
            Let r = (h.reservation - h.reservation@pre)->
            asSequence->first in
                -- returned ref is ref of the new reservation
                r.resRef = resRef and
                -- other attributes match
                r.dates = res.dateRange and
                r.roomType.name = res.roomType and not r.claimed and
                r.customer.id = cus
```

This looks pretty complicated, but if you follow the comments you should be able to see what's going on. Notice the use of @pre to refer to the set of reservations that the hotel had before the operation started. The ->as Sequence->first in piece is an idiom in OCL that allows us to extract the single member of a set from that set.

We have only described the success case so far. We cover alternative outcomes, errors, and exceptions in Chapter 8, where we discuss issues with mapping specifications to different target technologies and the use of multiple pre- and postconditions.

7.2.4   Exactly What Does a Postcondition Guarantee?

Strictly, if an effect is not specified in a postcondition, nothing is guaranteed about it. One of the reasons for this is to allow partial specification and subsequent specializations (i.e., subtypes) to fill in the details. However, if interpreted literally this means that every aspect of an object's state must be explicitly specified in the postcondition or else be undefined. But for practical purposes we don't want to have to say x=x@pre (i.e., no change) for every unreferenced element of the interface information model, so we recommend following these guidelines:

- If the precondition is true, anything not mentioned in the postcondition is assumed to be unchanged.

- If the precondition is false, the effect really is undefined, and you can make no assumptions about what might have changed and what hasn't.

These guidelines limit specialization and may worry purists, but they are simple and intuitive and therefore more likely to be used.[3]

If you decide to follow these guidelines, it's worth stating them explicitly somewhere. Often this kind of thing is left implicit, which can cause problems when component development is outsourced or existing components are bought in, when the principles followed may vary.

---

3. The correct approach to this is to frame the operation explicitly by stating the set of model elements that are the subject of the operation specification. Then we may make no assumptions about any element not included in that set.

7.3 Specifying System Interfaces

It should now be clear that there is a systematic way of moving from the business type model to the information models of the business interfaces. But what about the system interfaces? They, too, need to be specified. As we saw in Chapter 6, in many cases the system interface operations simply forward a call to the appropriate business interface. However, knowledge about those interactions does not form part of the usage contract of the system interface. A system interface—just like a business interface—must be specified in terms of its local interface information model.

As with any other interface, the interface information model of a system interface needs to contain just enough information to allow the operations to be specified. This will be a subset of the business type model.

It's important to understand that the existence of an interface information model does not imply that an implementation of the interface must store the information persistently. In fact, system interfaces rarely have persistent storage. Their implementations obtain the information they need from business components, but exactly how they do that is not important to the client of the system interface. We show later in this chapter how to specify the bindings between the information models of different interfaces.

As with business interfaces, we start by assuming that a system interface needs a copy of everything in the business type model. However, unlike business interfaces, where the interface responsibility diagram gives a clear indication of which types are needed by an interface and which are not, it might not be obvious which information types you need until you've specified the operations.

As you can see from Figure 7.6, the information model for IMakeReservation doesn't require the room number attribute, so that has been removed. On the other hand, the information model for ITakeUpReservation (see Figure 7.7) does require the room number but doesn't require the hotel name or the available(during) attribute of RoomType.

We specify each interface separately, hence the two separate diagrams, Figures 7.6 and 7.7. However, because these two system interfaces are closely related, they have very similar information models, and creating

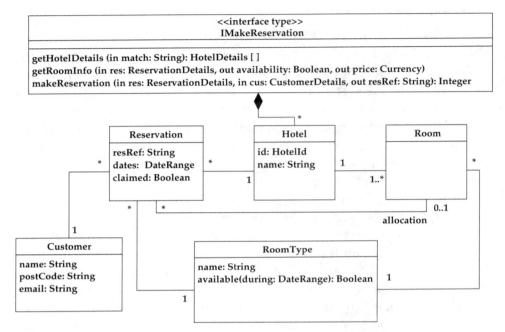

Figure 7.6 Interface specification diagram for IMakeReservation

and maintaining both is a lot of work. We can reduce the work we have to do by refactoring these interfaces, as described later in this chapter.

7.3.1 Business Rule Location

In Chapter 5 we showed how you can attach business rules (as invariants) to the business type model. These rules need to be restated in interface specifications so that they become part of the delivered software. The options for locating the business rules are:

- in the system interfaces only
- in the business interfaces only
- in both

Bear in mind that a business interface may be used in a variety of systems, fronted by different system interfaces. So if a rule is to apply in every situation it should be stated in the business interface. To avoid repetition, you might then

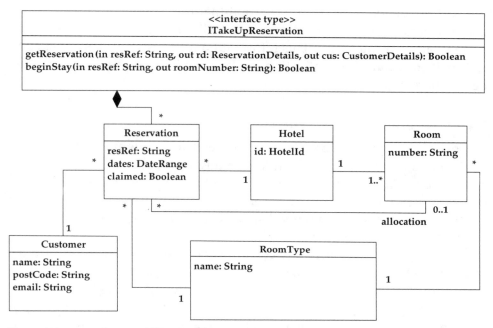

Figure 7.7   Interface specification diagram for ITakeUpReservation

not bother to state it in the system interface. This is fine if you want the rule to be invisible to clients of the system interface. If the rule is specific to a particular usage of the business interface it should be in the system interface only.

For example, consider the pricing policy in the case study. In the business type model we asserted the rule that the price for a stay is equal to the sum of the prices paid for individual nights. If we embed that rule in the IHotelMgt interface, it will apply to any system that uses that interface. If we embed it only in the IMakeReservation system interface, it will apply only the use of IHotel-Mgt in this particular system.

7.4   Specifying Components

The interface specifications discussed so far deal with the usage contract— the contract between a component object and its clients. Now we consider the additional specification information that the component implementer and assembler need to be aware of, especially the dependencies of a component on other interfaces. This information forms the component specification. If constraints on realization (and assembly) are to be specified, they belong here.

7.4.1   Offered and Used Interfaces

For every component specification we need to say which interfaces its realizations must support. We have already done this in the component architecture diagram in Chapter 5 (Figure 5.14), but we must dissect that diagram into pieces specific to each component spec. This is necessary because we want a self-contained specification package that we can hand to an implementer.

We also need to confirm any constraints concerning which other interfaces are to be used by a realization. Again, these constraints appeared on the component architecture diagram, as dependency arrows.

The component specification diagram for the hotel manager component shown in Figure 7.8 tells us that this component must offer the IHotelMgt interface and is not constrained to use any other interfaces. On the other hand, the component specification diagram for the reservation system component shown in Figure 7.9 tells us that this component must offer the two system interfaces and must use the three other interfaces. It doesn't, of course, tell us exactly how implementations of the component must use those interfaces—we'll come to that in a moment.

As well as showing a usage dependency on interfaces, a component specification diagram can show precisely how many component objects that offer the used interfaces are used by this component. We've already seen such a diagram in Chapter 6—it appears again in Figure 7.10.

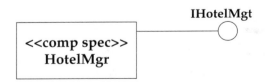

Figure 7.8   Component specification diagram for HotelMgr

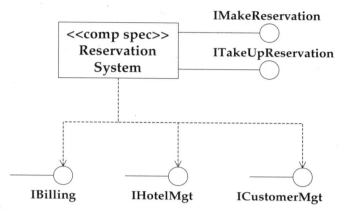

Figure 7.9 Component specification diagram for ReservationSystem

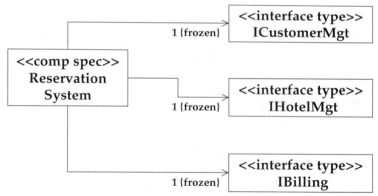

Figure 7.10 Additional component specification diagram for ReservationSystem

The diagram in Figure 7.10 tells us that all realizations of Reservation System must use exactly one component object offering each of the three interfaces, and that they will always be the same objects throughout the lifetime of the reservation system object (that's what the {frozen} constraint means).

7.4.2 Component Interaction Constraints

Constraints on how a particular operation must be implemented are defined in interactions. Unlike traditional implementation-level interactions, component interactions define specification-level constraints. All component realizations must respect them. This is essential if we aim to be able to replace components within a complex assembly. We can't have different realizations making completely different choices about how the application hangs together.

The interactions that make up the constraints on component specifications are typically fragments of the interactions we drew during operation discovery. They are the fragments that begin with a component object, of the kind being specified, receiving a message, and show *only* the direct interactions from that component. Figure 7.11 illustrates this.

The whole interaction was drawn to help discover operations, but now we want to specify component A. In that context we don't care about component B, and we don't care that the IX interface being used by A is

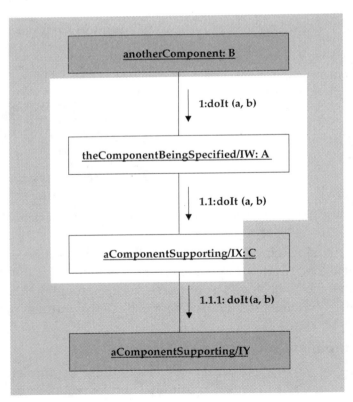

Figure 7.11 Scoping an interaction

being offered by component C. Since A isn't directly interacting with IY, we don't care about that interface, either.

The unshaded fragment specifies what a component object of type A must do when it receives the doIt( ) message via its IW interface. We include a fragment like this for each operation whose implementation we want to constrain. It isn't necessary to constrain the implementation of every operation—sometimes we can leave the details to the component designer.

Well, that's the theory. Unfortunately, most UML tools don't let you break a collaboration diagram into fragments. You'll either have to copy the diagrams and edit out the bits you don't want, or just put a copy of the whole thing into the component's specification package.

7.4.3   Inter-Interface Constraints

We aren't quite finished yet. There are two more things we might want to say about a component specification, both concerning the relationships between interface information models. The first concerns how the *offered* interfaces relate to each other, the second concerns how they relate to the *used* interfaces.

Offered Interfaces

The Reservation System component offers the IMakeReservation and the ITakeUpReservation interfaces. Both these interfaces have a Reservation information type. Since the two interfaces are specified completely independently, we can't assume that the reservations created by the component object via the IMakeReservation interface are the same reservations that can be found via the ITakeUpReservation interface. This may seem obvious in this case, but it isn't always obvious, and we should make it explicit. Sometimes we find information types in two offered interfaces with the same name that don't refer to the same concept, so it pays to be precise.

We add textual constraints to the component specification to ensure that the offered interfaces are implemented consistently:

```
context ReservationSystem
-- constraints between offered interfaces
IMakeReservation::hotel = ITakeUpReservation::hotel
IMakeReservation::reservation = ITakeUpReservation::reservation
IMakeReservation::customer = ITakeUpReservation::customer
```

The meaning of "=" here is that the instances of the information type in the first interface information model are logically the same as the instances of the information type in the second interface information model. A more formal definition of "=" depends on the two information types involved. For example, if they have common attributes it may mean that the value of these attributes is the same.

Offered Interfaces and Used Interfaces

Earlier in this chapter we pointed out that the existence of an interface information model in a system interface, such as IMakeReservation, does not imply that implementations of the interface will store that information; they obtain the information they need from business components, such as CustomerMgr. Rather than specifying that information retrieval in terms of messages sent from Reservation System (which offers IMakeReservation) to ICustomerMgt, we simply write constraints that require the elements of the interface information models to match up:

```
context ReservationSystem
-- constraints between offered interfaces and used interfaces
IMakeReservation::hotel = IHotelMgt::hotel
IMakeReservation::reservation = IHotelMgt::reservation
IMakeReservation::customer = ICustomerMgt::customer
```

These constraints tell implementers of Reservation System they need to ensure that the information they use to satisfy the postconditions of the offered operations matches the information described in the business interfaces. Of course, one implication of this is that the business interfaces offer operations suitable for that purpose, so that the information can be accessed. In this example, the constraints are satisfied by using the interactions we created in Chapter 6.

7.5   Factoring Interfaces

Creating all the interface information models can be hard work. Each interface needs its own model, which is often only slightly different from the model of another interface. Fortunately, it is sometimes possible to simplify things by refactoring the interfaces, especially by introducing new abstract interfaces that act as super-types of other interfaces, holding common interface information model elements, and, sometimes, definitions of common operations.

For example, it would be possible in the case study to factor out the common elements of the information models from IMakeReservation and ITakeUpReservation and place them in a new interface, called IReservationSystem, from which both inherit. IReservationSystem would then have an interface information model shown in Figure 7.12.

The interface information model for IMakeReservation then merely extends the inherited types, adding the extra attributes that are required (see Figure 7.13).

In some cases it may be practical simply to merge system interfaces together and not to bother with subtyping. This may be appropriate when the use cases to which these system interfaces correspond have the same actors. If they have different actors, it is important to maintain the separation to preserve the distinction between the different interfaces with the

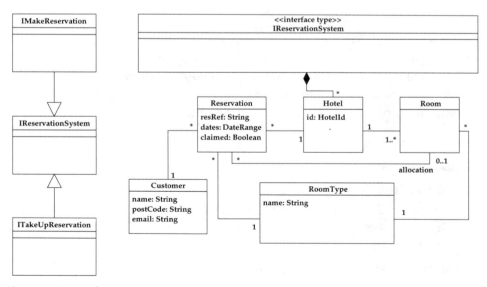

Figure 7.12 Refactoring interfaces

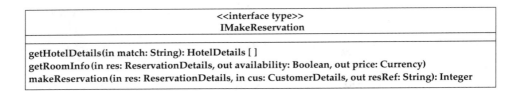

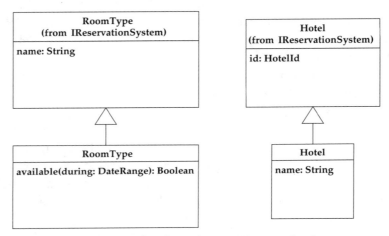

Figure 7.13   IMakeReservation after factoring out IReservationSystem

system—it allows for the other system functionality to vary as required. For example, the user interface, user dialog, access rights, and performance requirements of guests, reservation makers, and reservation administrators may vary. Keeping system interfaces separate facilitates the implementation of these different requirements.

7.6   Summary

We have covered a lot of detail in this chapter, and we've put in quite a bit of OCL, which you may not be familiar with. Let's take a step back and recap on the essential themes of our approach:

- Interface specifications define usage contracts.
- Component specifications define realization contracts.

- An interface is specified by a set of operation specifications that operate on an interface information model.

- The interface information model must contain just enough information to allow the operations to be specified. It cannot refer to anything outside the interface.

- First-cut interface information models can be derived systematically from the business type model.

- Each operation is specified using a pre- and postcondition pair. The postcondition defines the effects of the operation, while the precondition defines the conditions under which the postcondition is guaranteed.

- OCL is a useful declarative language for writing invariants and operation pre- and postconditions. It's hard work to use, but offers greater precision. Whether you use a formal language or not, *always* write the natural language versions—don't make assumptions.

- Component specifications include specifications of the interfaces offered and used. They can also include details about the number of component objects expected.

- To constrain the implementations of operations, attach interaction fragments to component specifications.

- Add constraints to component specifications to define how elements in one interface information model relate to elements in another.

- Consider factoring or merging system interfaces to keep things simple, but bear in mind the value of different actors having their own interfaces on the system.

This chapter completes our explanation of the specification workflow, which is the main subject of this book. We now finish by touching briefly on some of the key issues when moving to component provisioning and assembly, and deal with some more complicated topics that we put to one side earlier.

Chapter 8

Provisioning and Assembly

U p to this point we have concentrated on creating specifications of components. In this chapter we look beyond specification at some of the issues involved in provisioning components to meet the required specification. We also summarize some of the key goals of the assembly workflow.

The purpose of the provisioning workflow, mentioned briefly in Chapter 2, is to source component implementations, either by directly implementing the specification or by finding an existing component that fits the specification.

We have tried to make sure that the component specifications we create are as independent as possible from the idiosyncrasies of the target technologies. However, some specification techniques are not directly supported by all target technologies, so a certain amount of interpretation is required. We now look at where certain technologies differ and how this affects the mapping from specification to implementation.

8.1 What Do We Mean by Target Technology?

When we use the term *target technology* we are principally referring to the runtime component environment. We also include in this the implementation language, but it is of secondary importance.

In this context, a **Component Environment** is a distributed object environment, together with a set of rules to which components must conform—a component standard—to operate in that environment, and a set of infrastructure services (transaction support, security, concurrency, and so on) on which the application component can depend. Further, we restrict ourselves to those component environments that provide these infrastructure services declaratively, using a framework approach (sometimes called "attribute-based programming"), rather than through explicit invocation by the application logic itself. This is because these environments are the most suited to providing a firm base for the next generation of distributed, enterprise-scale, component-based applications. In today's world what this boils down to is a fairly stark set of options:

Component Environment	Platform Dependencies	Language Dependencies
Microsoft COM+ (COM+)	Windows 2000	None
Enterprise JavaBeans (EJB)	None	Java

This isn't a book about the state and direction of the component environment market, so we're not going to start analyzing the relative merits of these two technologies. Apart from platform and language dependencies, another interesting difference is that COM+ comes from a single vendor and is a piece of software, not a specification, whereas EJB is a specification standard agreed on by a large number of companies and is not software. In any event, many enterprise-scale application development projects will find themselves having to deal with both of these, so we will too.

At this point we should also mention the CCM because it is an emerging component environment that satisfies our component environment criteria and has the potential to rank alongside COM+ and EJB. However, since CCM is still under development, we'll just look at COM+ and EJB.

In the specification workflow we have been working in a technology-independent way. In practice, the chosen provisioning technology is often known in advance, at least for some of the components. With this in mind it is useful to identify those areas where the specifications must accommodate particular constraints to enable a clean mapping to the implementation technology. We've tried to highlight those areas here. Conceptually, COM+ and EJB actually have a great deal in common. They differ in the details.

8.2 Components Realize Component Specifications

Let's just recap on our UML relationships. In UML as it stands, a component realizes one or more interfaces. As we've discussed before, this is sufficient to model some of the implementation technology details of components. To handle specification we've added some UML stereotypes to introduce the «comp spec» class, and the notion of «interface type». A component specification offers one or more interface types. We therefore have a fairly simple correspondence between the specification constructs and the implementation ones: A component realizes a component specification and an interface realizes an interface type (see Figure 8.1).

UML also defines the relationship between a component and an interface as a «realize» relationship (and that's how we've shown it in the diagram), but it isn't really a form of abstraction and is more akin to our «offers» relationship.

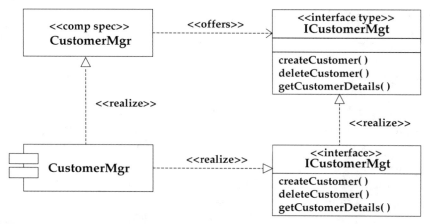

Figure 8.1 Implementations realize specifications

From a provisioning point of view, we consider what mappings need to take place for these two key realizations, between the technology-neutral level and the technology-specific level, and which are the main areas to watch.

8.3   Realization Mappings and Restrictions

The main issues with mapping to a target technology arise from the following considerations:

- Operation parameter type, kind (in/out/inout/return), and reference restrictions
- Exception and error handling mechanisms
- Interface inheritance and support restrictions
- Operation sequence
- Interface properties
- Object creation mechanisms
- Raising events

We'll deal briefly which each of these in turn.

8.3.1   Operation Parameters

Both EJB and COM+ are distributed component environments. Each uses a mechanism for invoking operations on remote objects. This involves bundling the operation parameters up into a stream, squirting them around, and unbundling them again, in a process called "marshalling." One implication of this is that parameters can only be of two kinds: either data, which is passed by value (the information is copied), or objects, which are passed by reference (i.e., they're not passed at all, but a reference to the object is supplied). So regardless of your implementation language, you must keep to these two kinds of parameter in your operations.

In EJB, the operation invocation mechanism is called Java Remote Method Invocation (JRMI). All parameters must follow the JRMI rules; in particular, this means that parameters passed by value must be serializable. One important consequence of using JRMI is that it isn't possible to implement out parameters directly; all outputs must be returned via the operation result.

COM+ is implementation-language-neutral—it is a binary standard. This means, for example, that a COM+ component implemented in Java can call another implemented in C++. For this to work there needs to be a standard data type mapping between the common implementation languages. So far so good. Now COM+ provides a special mechanism called "automation" for discovering and invoking operations at runtime, through a standardized interface. This is the mechanism used by its popular Visual Basic for Applications (VBA) language to invoke operations, with lots of nice syntactic sugar thrown in. This means that any operation that needs to be made available through the COM+ automation mechanism needs to use parameter types that will map onto the types used by VBA. Refer to COM+ documentation for a full list of these.

8.3.2   Error and Exception Handling Mechanisms

Pre- and postconditions describe the assumed initial states and guaranteed resultant states of an object following an operation execution. Since there may be a variety of possible initial states, with corresponding resultant states, it is natural to consider specifying these possible possibilities as separate pre- and postcondition pairs.

Returning to our IHotelMgt::getReservation() operation, we have defined a pre- and postcondition pair for the case where a reservation exists and it has not already been claimed. Under some circumstances this would be a sufficiently complete specification of the operation. However, we might decide to specify the behavior of the operation under other conditions too. For example, what happens when the reservation number supplied cannot be found, or when it has already been claimed?

One way to handle these cases is to extend UML and have a pre- and postcondition pair for each combination. For example (using natural language for brevity):

```
context IHotelMgt::getReservation(
        in resRef: String,
        out rd: ReservationDetails,
        out cus: CustId): Integer

-- "Normal" case
pre:  -- a reservation corresponding to resRef exists and it
      -- hasn't been claimed
post: -- result = 0, reservation details and customer ID returned

-- "Reservation Not Found" case
pre:  -- a reservation corresponding to resRef does not exist
post: -- result = 1, return an appropriate reason code and message string

-- "Already Claimed" case
pre:  -- the reservation has been claimed
post: -- result = 2, return an appropriate reason code and message string
```

There's nothing to stop you specifying the preconditions in a way that will allow two or more of them to be true simultaneously. If you do that take care to ensure that the corresponding postconditions don't define inconsistent outcomes.

This approach has been adopted successfully in [Advisor], and is described by D'Souza [D'Souza99] under the heading "multiple action specifications." It fits well with COM+, where each operation is a function that returns a standard result structure. This structure can be used to indicate the effect of the operation, including normal and exception cases.

EJB is based on Java and uses the exception mechanism built into the language. You will need to decide how your specification maps onto this exception handling approach. Exceptions are effectively a special way of handling certain types of operation effect. First you need to make a decision about your error handling philosophy: Will you use exceptions only to imply a departure from an operation's specified contract (following [Meyer97]), or do exceptions represent expected, defined behavior? If the former, you would always use return parameters to hold resultant states described in pre- and postconditions, as in the example, and the exceptions would not be specified. If the latter, you need a way of mapping postconditions to exceptions.

One approach, based on that proposed by Soundarajan and Fridella [Soundarajan99], is to mark the postconditions with the exception they raise, in the form of a declaration:

```
context IHotelMgt::getReservation(
    in resRef: String,
    out rd: ReservationDetails,
    out cus: CustId)

-- "Normal" case
norm.pre:           -- a reservation corresponding to resRef exists
                    -- and it hasn't been claimed
norm.post:          -- reservation details and customer ID returned

-- "Reservation Not Found" case
NotFoundException.pre:
                    -- a reservation corresponding to resRef
                    -- does not exist
nf:NotFoundException.post:
                    -- the attributes of the NotFoundException object nf
                    -- are set to indicate the nature of the failure

-- "Already Claimed" case
AlreadyClaimedException.pre:
                    -- the reservation has been claimed
ac:AlreadyClaimedException.post:
                    -- the attributes of the AlreadyClaimedException
                    -- object ac are set to indicate the nature of the
                    -- failure
```

Using this approach it is possible to indicate the exception raised and show the required values for the exception's attributes.

What is the best way to extend UML to handle multiple pre- and postconditions? UML allows multiple constraints to be attached to any object, so this means multiple individual pre- and postconditions can be attached to an operation. What is missing is some way of pairing them up. A variety of approaches are possible:

1. Use a naming convention in the body of each constraint (probably the simplest and most practical approach).

2. Have a single precondition, with multiple postconditions, each including the appropriate distinguishing precondition case. Then no pairing is needed.

3. Have multiple operations with the same name and signature, and combine them to create the full specification, as described in Catalysis.

8.3.3   Interface Inheritance and Interface Support

There is a significant difference between COM+ and EJB when it comes to interface inheritance and support.

COM+ only allows single interface inheritance. To allow objects to have multiple classifications, components can support multiple interfaces. For example, a COM+ document object could be a document, and an invoice, and an account statement, by supporting IDocument, IInvoice, and IAccStmnt. Additionally, all COM+ interfaces must ultimately inherit from IUnknown—the base COM+ interface.

Java allows multiple interface inheritance and allows Java classes to support multiple interfaces, while only allowing single class inheritance. This is the good news. The bad news is that when registering a Java class as an EJB with an EJB component environment, you are restricted to naming one interface (the so-called remote interface). The container for your EJB provides a class supporting this interface, which then delegates to your Java class. Although your Java class could support many interfaces, the EJB container, and hence the client, can only know about one of them. This means that if you want your component to support multiple interfaces you'll need to use multiple interface inheritance to pull all the component's functionality under one umbrella interface, which can be registered with the EJB environment. This super interface is effectively acting as the component specification.

Take care when using inheritance with interface types. Since these are specification artifacts, defining contracts, inheritance behaves additively. Unlike implementation class inheritance where subclass methods can override superclass methods, subtype operation specifications can only augment the contract defined by their super-types. If you have a design-by-contract view of the world then this is akin to subcontracting—a contract can be subcontracted only if the subcontract conforms to the assumptions and guarantees of the original contract. More specifically this means that when specializing operations you may weaken the precondition (make it less stringent) and strengthen the postcondition (make it more stringent). This ensures that any client dependent on the assumptions and guarantees of the super-type will not find the subtype behaving in an unexpected way. (This is an interesting and rather complex area: see [Cook94], [Meyer97], and [D'Souza99] for more details).

8.3.4   Operation Sequence

COM+ is a binary standard and operation references rely on memory off-sets based on the order in which operations are specified in the interface. Thus, in COM+, operation order is significant. If a client depends on a certain operation order you cannot change it. So don't start sorting your operations alphabetically, or into logical groups, once you have any client code dependencies. When the interface is upgraded using inheritance, any new operations are added at the end of the list.

8.3.5   Interface Properties

In COM+ an interface property is specification shorthand for a get and set pair of operations. If you are using UML to specify interfaces as described in Chapter 3, an interface attribute exists purely for supporting the specification of pre- and postconditions of operations, and you must explicitly define which operations you want. For example, the base COM+ interface IUnknown has two operations for managing reference counts: addref( ) and release( ). The specification of these operations needs to refer to the interface attribute "reference count," but in COM+ defining such an attribute would indirectly define the existence of operations to access that value directly (which is not what we want to specify).

So, for mapping to COM+, we need a way to determine which operations should map onto the COM+ property shorthand. One simple way is to use a naming convention (as in JavaBeans—but not EJB). Alternatively you could be more elaborate and extend your operation specification with a tagged value for the property name, and interpret from the existence of in or out parameters to determine which was the get and which was the set.

8.3.6   Object Creation

Both EJB and COM+ use an object factory approach where one component object is used to create instances of another component. In EJB the factory is the Home object, in COM+ it is the IClassFactory[1] object. In component architecture diagrams and component object interactions it

---

1. IObjectFactory might have been a better name for this.

can be convenient to omit this level of indirection and simply show «create» dependencies directly to the component object itself. When mapping to the component environment, this indirection detail needs to be added in, so your implementation-level interaction diagrams need to show it.

In COM+ there is a lot of flexibility about which object is the factory. It is simply a designated component that offers the relevant IClassFactory for a given class. It may also do other things, and you must deliver an implementation of it. For EJB session beans you need only provide a specification (and not an implementation) of the I<...>Home interface, but for entity beans you need to provide the implementation as well.

8.3.7   Raising Events

COM+ has an event model where an interface for a given COM+ class can be specified as outgoing. What this means is that instead of the component offering the interface, it expects other components to offer it, and will invoke operations of this interface to signal events or significant changes in state. The outgoing interface therefore acts as a sink or destination for an event signal. The component that is the source of the event offers a separate interface to allow for registration of interest in that event.

This COM+ specification construct is effectively just a specialized usage of our more general semantics for component specifications. Because we define both offered and used interfaces in our specification of components, this special COM+ feature needs no additional modeling— the outgoing interface is a used interface, as shown in Figure 8.2.

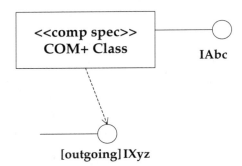

Figure 8.2   Outgoing interface

8.4 Application Architecture Correspondence

We have proposed a number of distinct layers in the architecture of application, with each layer having different responsibilities (see Figure 8.3). We now indicate briefly how certain specification features of these layers could map to the target technologies. Clearly the detailed considerations of architecting systems in a particular component technology is a book in itself, so we limit ourselves to a few general observations on the use of session and entity EJBs (this distinction does not exist in COM+) and which transaction properties to use.

The dialog software layer is responsible for managing the dialog with the user. It need not be componentized at all—it could be any lump of software—but it may well need to hold and manage the state of the dialog.

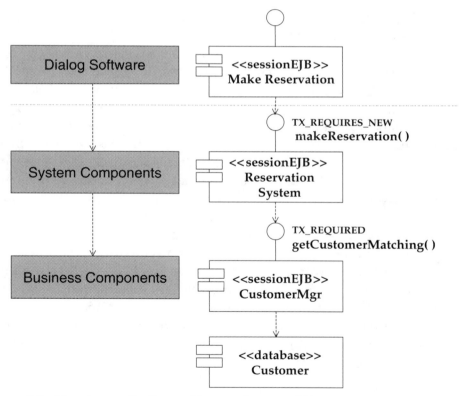

Figure 8.3 Mapping application architecture layers to EJB

If it were a component in EJB it would correspond to a stateful session EJB. It is a session bean because its state is exclusive to the user dialog it supports and so should not be shared.

System components offer interfaces whose operations are business transactions, and we marked them «transaction» in the specification. In EJB this would correspond to TX_REQUIRES_NEW. Since system component interfaces correspond to use cases, and represent the system's responsibilities in the dialog with the user, they do not need to be shared; therefore they are also modeled as session EJBs and are typically stateless[2] (the dialog software manages the dialog state and the business components handle the business state).

8.4.1   Business Components

Business components offer interfaces whose operations are part of a business transaction. They are not typically standalone transactions themselves. In EJB this case would correspond to TX_REQUIRED.

When we derive business components from the business type model, we tend to choose the manager interfaces and components, such as CustomerMgr, which manage large numbers of instances of business types. To access and process those instances, clients of the manager component typically have to pass instance identifiers of some sort to the manager interface operations. When implementing these manager business components directly in EJB, we use a session bean, so that each client has its own customer manager (a session bean component object) and the sharing and transaction control of the underlying instances is managed by the database.

This approach is the simple choice, applicable in many cases, and allows you to support an interface exactly as specified. The drawbacks are that you will have to provide your own persistence code, with a resource overhead for each manager, and the possible lack of in-memory data sharing, which might hurt performance. An alternative, which is used frequently in COM+, is to continue to apply the component model below the level of the manager, surfacing the individual managed instances in the form of component objects.

---

2. Or have constant state.

For example, rather than ICustomerMgt offering a getCustomerDetails( ) operation and taking a variety of instance identifying details (see Figure 8.4) it could instead surface Customers as objects in their own right (see Figure 8.5). They would look and feel like component objects from the point of view of the client code, and would simplify the specification of some of the functionality of the manager interface because there would be less need to dereference instances. Operations specific to a single instance can be defined on an interface which represents that interface.

In this approach we can use an EJB entity bean to implement the ICustomer interface, where each entity bean instance represents one customer. This allows you to use container-managed persistence for retrieval and storage of the customer structures.

There are some points to bear in mind in following this approach. First, this approach can be very inefficient if, for example, a client iterates over a collection of ICustomer objects, performing a simple operation on each one. It does makes sense if a sequence of complex operations are to be applied to a single customer, or if the cost of invocation is low. Second, we still need a manager, for creation at least. In EJB it is possible for the Home bean to act as manager, providing the simple management operations required. However, if you need to provide batch operations that act

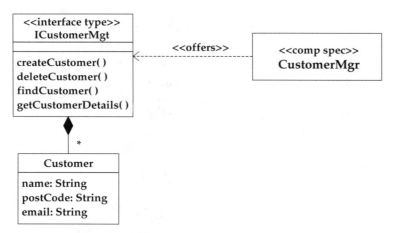

Figure 8.4 Encapsulated customers

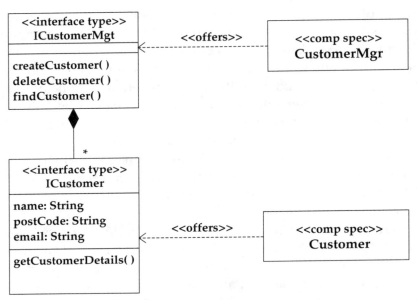

Figure 8.5   Explicit modeling of customers

on a set of instances, to improve performance, the manager will need to be a separate component that is located physically close to the Customer component (probably in the same container).

A third possibility for implementing business components in EJB is to use entity bean component objects to represent a set of instances. With this approach we use a finder operation on the CustomerSet Home to create a component object that represents the set of customers we want to operate on. Then we use the operations of this customer-set object to work with the set all at once. This approach allows for a variety of component object granularities, either through explicit operations returning specific customer subsets, or under client control, through suitable filtering parameters.

8.5   Subcomponents

A component specification is a packaging of functionality (in the form of one or more interfaces) corresponding to a single implementation unit. It defines the unit of provisioning and replacement in the application architecture. Often the provisioning and replacement granularity requirements for a large-scale business application give rise to quite coarse-grained components. Manager components fit well with this.

However, sometimes we want to expose a richer object model to the client, as we did with customers in our case study, without introducing a myriad of separate components, each acting as its own provisioning and replacement unit. As another example, consider the HotelMgr component of our case study. We might want to expose hotels, rooms, room types, and reservations as component objects directly to clients, but we don't want to end up with four or five separate components.

How do we balance the need to define a relatively coarse-grained component for provisioning purposes with the specification and usage simplicity that derives from finer-grained components?

To address this problem we can mark component specifications as sub-components (using a «sub comp spec» stereotype), and relate them to a containing normal component specification (see Figure 8.6). The difference is that these subcomponents are not encapsulation boundaries and do not represent separately replaceable units. They expose a cleaner programming model to the client code while allowing implementation efficiencies to be made by sharing implementation details between subcomponents of the

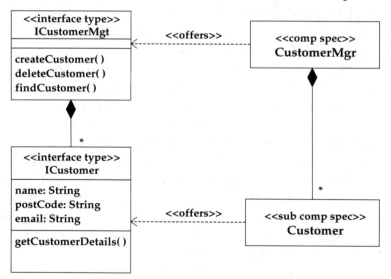

Figure 8.6   Manager component with finer-grained subcomponents

same component. The CustomerMgr and Customer components must be replaced as a single unit.

Another case for taking a subcomponent approach is when you have components in your architecture that you had intended to develop, replace, and manage separately, but the interaction between them is such that you decide you need the performance advantages of a single implementation. The subcomponent approach allows you to maintain the specification structuring that you had (from a client point of view) while adopting a coarser-grained approach to implementation and deployment.

Subcomponents do not have explicit factory objects in the way that true components do. Instead, their instances are created by specific operations of the parent component or sibling subcomponents. For example, the ICustomerMgt::createCustomer( ) operation would create a instance of the Customer subcomponent. Subcomponent objects share state with their containing component and only exist at runtime. They are not a deployment-time concept. A component and all its subcomponents must be packaged together into the same module (.exe, .dll, .jar).

8.6 Integrating Existing Systems

Although we have drawn our architecture diagrams showing neat, well-defined components, in reality much of the functionality for a business application is drawn from existing systems. This is mainly due to the need to leverage the substantial investments that have been made in these systems, and the business intelligence they contain, as well as the need to assemble new solutions quickly. The time-to-market imperative of e-business applications doesn't usually permit lengthy redesigns.

This topic deserves a book in itself, so we don't aim to do it justice here but simply to show how existing systems would feature in our component architectures and how their characteristics don't provide all of the sought-after change management objectives. Simply sticking a component-technology face onto an existing system doesn't mean you're suddenly "doing components" or following a component approach.

Sometimes code can be recovered using invasive legacy mining, but more often functionality will be reused in a noninvasive way via the API of the existing system or enterprise application integration (EAI) software. We used the Billing System in our case study as an example of such a system, and we assumed the use of an adapter to provide a bridge between the component environment being used and the system being invoked behind the scenes.

Whether you are using explicit adapters, EAI integration software, or accessing existing APIs, specifying the services provided by the existing system in the form of an interface with an interface information model will greatly aid usage, testing, and staged migration of functionality. The interface information models for an adapter represent the concepts managed by the legacy system, but expressed in the vocabulary of the architectural context in which it is being used. It is useful to define clear correspondences between the information type names and the concepts and parameters used by the legacy system, and to define any constraints that exist. Inevitably, part of the effort of reusing an existing system is in re-establishing a clear specification of the system operations, constraints, and so on.

Although existing systems can be adapted to look like components, they typically fail one of the defining criteria—encapsulation—because they generally continue to be used in other contexts; that is, they are not used exclusively via the adapter. When using such components it is important to be aware of any side-effects that you may be relying on that are not part of the adapter specification, and which may cause failure if the legacy adaptation approach for provisioning that component were replaced by a new implementation. For example, you may assume the state of certain attributes to have default values when instances are first created, because this is what the current system does. It is important to make sure all these behavioral characteristics are specified, otherwise future implementations may not respect them.

8.7 Purchasing Components

The dream of reusing off-the-shelf components has taken longer to materialize than first envisaged. It seems to have been "a year away" since around the mid-1990s. With the emergence of UML for standardizing on design-time details, and COM+ and EJB for (semi-) standardizing on the runtime technology, the industry is genuinely poised for large-scale reuse now to become a reality. In turn this places extra emphasis on the need for thorough and precise specifications.

The organizational and process discipline needed to adopt a component approach within a company can be difficult to achieve. If the person implementing the component is in the same building as the one specifying it, inevitably some of the details of what the component needs to do, and how it should behave, will go via the coffee room and may not quite make it into the specification model. And if they're not in the specification, the component tester will probably need to have a quick word with the implementer, too.

Development teams talking to each other is a good thing. The problem is that, as a process, it doesn't scale very well, so relying on it for correct system behavior will get you in trouble. When we bring multiple organizations into the picture it gets even harder. This is why we've placed so much emphasis on specification. When dealing with high-functionality coarse-grained components, and inter-company contracts, it is essential.

Detailed and precise specifications serve two purposes when you are searching for off-the-shelf components in a catalog. First they define what you are looking for. Second they define what the component in the catalog actually does. The problem then is to tie the two together, referred to by some as *gap analysis*. Like the integration of existing systems, the reuse of existing components may be driven bottom-up as well as top-down. If you know there is a component out there that does some of what you want, you'll plan to use it in advance and define the adapter as part of the provisioning process.

8.8　Assembly

Assembly is the process of pulling together components and existing software assets into a working system, and designing a user interface for that system, based on the use case models, to form an application (see Figure 8.7).

Assembly shares many characteristics with standard configuration management practices. Each individual component, or integrated existing

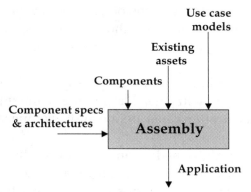

Figure 8.7 The Assembly workflow

asset, can be viewed as a separate configuration item, under version control. The component architecture represents the system configuration definition—what the required configuration items are and what their dependencies are. It is the model equivalent of the *make file* at the programming level, and assembly is analogous to build.

Assembly is also responsible for defining the user interface and the user dialog logic (recall from Chapter 1 that we treat these as separate layers within the application architecture). The user dialog logic is designed according to the use cases in the use case model.

The application is passed to the test workflow for system and user acceptance testing.

8.9 Summary

The choice of target technology will affect the way you map specifications to implementations. Each technology will have its own restrictions and limitations. Areas where mappings are required include

- parameter passing
- error and exception handling mechanisms
- interface inheritance and interface support

Decisions about the granularity of the object model exposed to clients must be made. These decisions determine the way the target technology is used to realize business components, such as the choice between session and entity beans in EJB.

Subcomponent specifications can be used to support the definition of finer-grained usage contracts with the client, while maintaining coarser-grained component specifications that define provisioning and replacement boundaries.

Components may be provisioned by implementing the specification, or integrating existing software through both invasive and noninvasive approaches, or by purchasing the component off-the-shelf from a catalog or a business partner.

Assembly pulls the application together, using the component architecture for the system to define the overall structure and the individual pieces, and adding user interface and user dialog logic.

Then it's a small matter of testing and deployment. But we'll stop here.

8.10   A Final Thought

The only constant in application development is that things will change. Carefully followed processes and good people can produce quality applications that meet the business requirement. But they cannot stop the business requirement from changing.

We hope that by taking a component-based approach, and paying particular attention to specification and architecture, you'll be better positioned to create robust but adaptable applications in a cost-effective way, to enable your organizations to survive in this increasingly competitive and rapidly changing world.

References

[Advisor]
Sterling Software Component-Based Development Method (available with COOL:Spex and COOL:Gen products), http://www.sterling.com/cool and http://www.ca.com/products

[Beck99]
Beck, K. *Extreme Programming Explained—Embrace Change,* Addison-Wesley, 2000.

[CCM]
CORBA Component Model, http://www.omg.org/techprocess/ meetings/schedule/CORBA_Component_Model_RFP.html

[Cockburn00]
Writing Effective Use Cases, http://members.aol.com/humansandt/crystal/ usecasetechnique/getWEUCbook.htm

[CockburnWeb]
http://members.aol.com/acockburn/

[COM+]
Microsoft COM+, http://msdn.microsoft.com

[Constantine99]
Constantine, L., and L. Lockwood. *Software for Use—A Practical Guide to the Models and Methods of Usage-Centered Design,* Addison-Wesley, 1999.

[Cook94]
Cook, S., and J. Daniels. *Designing Object Systems,* Prentice Hall, 1994.

[D'Souza99]
D'Souza, D. F., and A. C. Wills. *Objects, Components, and Frameworks with UML: The Catalysis^{SM} Approach,* Addison-Wesley, 1999.

[DSDM]
Dynamic Systems Development Method, http://www.dsdm.org/

[EJB]
Enterprise JavaBeans, http://java.sun.com/products/ejb/

[Fowler99]
Fowler, M. *UML Distilled, Second Edition—A Brief Guide to the Standard Object Modeling Language*, Addison-Wesley, 2000.

[Gamma95]
Gamma, E. et al. *Design Patterns*, Addison-Wesley, 1995.

[Gilb88]
Gilb, T. *Principles of Software Engineering Management*, Addison-Wesley, 1988.

[GilbWeb]
http://www.result-planning.com

[Hodgson99]
"Systems Envisioning." Workshop at OOPSLA99, Denver, Colorado, November 1999.

[Jackson95]
Jackson, M. *Software Requirements & Specifications—A Lexicon of Practice, Principles, and Prejudices*, Addison-Wesley, 1995.

[Jacobson99]
Jacobson I. et. al., *The Unified Software Development Process*, Addison-Wesley, 1999.

[Kruchten99]
Kruchten, P. *The Rational Unified Process—An Introduction*, Addison-Wesley, 1999.

[Meyer97]
Meyer, B. *Object-Oriented Software Construction* (2nd ed.), Prentice Hall, 1997.

[OIM]
Metadata Corporation Open Information Model,
http://msdn.microsoft.com/repository/oim/ and
http://www.mdcinfo.com/OIM/documents.html

[Rumbaugh91]
Rumbaugh, J. et al. *Object-Oriented Modeling and Design*, Prentice Hall, 1991.

[Sellers99]
Henderson-Sellers, B., and F. Barbier. "Black and White Diamonds," paper presented at UML 99, Fort Collins, Colorado, October 1999.

[Soundarajan99]
Soundarajan, N., and S. Fridella. "Modeling Exceptional Behavior," paper presented at UML 99, Fort Collins, Colorado, October 1999.

[UML]
The Unified Modeling Language v1.3, Object Management Group,
http://www.omg-org/uml

[Warmer99]
Warmer, J., and A. Kleppe. *The Object Constraint Language—Precise Modeling with UML*, Addison-Wesley, 1999.

Index

Also Available from Addison-Wesley

The Object Constraint Language
Precise Modeling with UML
Jos Warmer and Anneke Kleppe
Addison-Wesley Object Technology Series

The Object Constraint Language is a notational language, a subset of the Unified Modeling Language that allows software developers to express a set of rules that govern very specific aspects of an object in object-oriented applications. With the OCL, developers are able to more easily express unique limitations and write the fine print that is often necessary in complex software designs. The authors' pragmatic approach and illustrative use of examples will help application developers to quickly get up to speed.

0-201-37940-6 • Paperback • 144 pages • ©1999

Software Project Management
A Unified Framework
Walker Royce
Addison-Wesley Object Technology Series
This book presents a new management framework uniquely suited to the complexities of modern software development. Walker Royce's pragmatic perspective exposes the shortcomings of many well-accepted management priorities and equips software professionals with state-of-the-art knowledge derived from his twenty years of successful from-the-trenches management experience. In short, this book provides the software industry with field-proven benchmarks for making tactical decisions and strategic choices that will enhance an organization's probability of success.

0-201-30958-0 • Hardcover • 448 pages • ©1998

Enterprise Computing with Objects
From Client/Server Environments to the Internet
Yen-Ping Shan and Ralph H. Earle
Addison-Wesley Object Technology Series

This book helps you place rapidly evolving technologies—such as the Internet, the World Wide Web, distributed computing, object technology, and client /server systems—in their appropriate contexts when preparing for the development, deployment, and maintenance of information systems. The authors distinguish what is essential from what is incidental, while imparting a clear understanding of how the underlying technologies fit together. This book examines essential topics, including data persistence, security, performance, scalability, and development tools.

0-201-32566-7 • Paperback • 448 pages • ©1998

Register
Your Book
at www.aw.com/cseng/register

You may be eligible to receive:
- Advance notice of forthcoming editions of the book
- Related book recommendations
- Chapter excerpts and supplements of forthcoming titles
- Information about special contests and promotions throughout the year
- Notices and reminders about author appearances, tradeshows, and online chats with special guests

Contact us

If you are interested in writing a book or reviewing manuscripts prior to publication, please write to us at:

Editorial Department
Addison-Wesley Professional
75 Arlington Street, Suite 300
Boston, MA 02116 USA
Email: AWPro@aw.com

Addison-Wesley

Visit us on the Web: http://www.aw.com/cseng